D1195737

Programming with APSE Software Tools

Programming with
APSE
Software Tools

Roy S. Freedman

PETROCELLI BOOKS
Princeton, New Jersey

Printed in the United States of America
First Printing

Composition by Eastern Graphics

Library of Congress Cataloging in Publication Data

Freedman, Roy S.
    Programming with APSE software tools.

    Bibliography: p.
    Includes index.
    1. Ada (Computer program language) 2. Electronic
digital computers—Programming. I. Title.
QA76.73.A35F74   1984   001.64'24   84-20739
ISBN 0-89433-220-1

Contents

PREFACE   vii

SECTION ONE   INTRODUCTION AND OVERVIEW   1

Chapter 1 WHAT IS AN APSE?   3
Chapter 2 WHY DO WE NEED AN APSE?   11
Chapter 3 WHAT ARE THE REQUIREMENTS FOR AN APSE?   27
Chapter 4 APSE COMPONENTS   39
Chapter 5 ADDENDUM: FORMAL SEMANTICS   47

SECTION TWO   ASPECTS OF CONTROL   53

Chapter 6 AN APSE DIALOG   55
Chapter 7 APSE CONTROL INTERFACE REQUIREMENTS   81
Chapter 8 COMMAND LANGUAGE PROCESSORS   89
Chapter 9 EDITORS AND INTEGRATED ENVIRONMENTS   103

SECTION THREE   DATA BASE ISSUES   111

Chapter 10 WHAT'S IN A PATHNAME?   113
Chapter 11 EXPRESSIONS FOR CONFIGURATION MANAGEMENT   131
Chapter 12 LIBRARY TOOLS   141
Chapter 13 HELP! WHAT DOES THIS TOOL DO?   149

SECTION FOUR   RUNTIME SUPPORT   155

Chapter 14 WHAT IS RUNTIME SUPPORT?   157
Chapter 15 RUNTIME SUPPORT TOOLS   163
Chapter 16 INCOMPLETE PROGRAMMING   175
Chapter 17 DISTRIBUTED PROGRAMMING   181
Chapter 18 DEBUGGING: TOOLS FOR QUALITY ASSURANCE   191

SECTION FIVE   INTERFACE ISSUES   203

Chapter 19 APSE INTERFACES   205
Chapter 20 WRITING APSE TOOLS IN ADA   211
Chapter 21 WHAT MAKES A KAPSE A KAPSE?   217

REFERENCES   223

APPENDIX   CAIS DRAFT 1.3 PACKAGE SPECIFICATIONS   229

INDEX   249

Preface

The Ada programming language was developed to aid the production of high-quality software for embedded computer applications. During the development of the Ada language, it was realized that special purpose software tools and resources were needed to provide support for Ada application programs that fully utilize the power of the Ada language. These tools and resources, called an Ada Programming Support Environment (APSE), consist of an integrated set of tools, data base facilities, and control interfaces. In this book, we show what an APSE is and how it may be used in the design, implementation, and maintenance of Ada application programs.

This book is divided into five sections, each corresponding to a different aspect of an APSE.

Section One reviews the general requirements associated with an APSE and provides a rationale for these requirements. The Stoneman model for an APSE is introduced and examined in detail. There is also a chapter on the application of denotational semantics for specifying certain APSE characteristics.

Section Two is concerned with the control and invocation of APSE resources. We present a user dialog with an APSE in a "typical" interactive programming session.

Section Three deals with APSE resource management. The APSE data base requirements and the CAIS node model are presented and applied to simple configuration management situations.

Section Four presents a detailed discussion of APSE compilers and linkers. APSE support for incomplete and distributed Ada programming is also closely examined. There is also a chapter in this section on tools for Ada software quality assurance.

Finally, Section Five examines the APSE from the viewpoint of Ada software portability. The use of a standard KAPSE interface in the development of portable APSE tools is studied.

The book is organized in a top-down fashion and is presented from the viewpoint of an APSE user. All sections begin with a chapter addressing requirements and conclude with chapters showing how these requirements can be met. All chapters conclude with an annotated set of references and a few exercises for the reader. We assume a familiarity with the Ada programming language; otherwise, the book is self-contained.

I would like to acknowledge the help of several people in the preparation of this book. I thank my colleagues from Working Group One of the KAPSE Interface Team Industry and Academia (KITIA). In particular, I thank Fred Cox, Anthony Gargaro, and Tim Lindquist for reading and commenting on my manuscripts. I also thank the remainder of my colleagues on the KIT and KITIA, and thank Tricia Oberndorf for bringing us together. Thanks also to Lt.Cmdr. Brian Schaar of the Ada Joint Program Office for his time in reading the manuscript.

At Hazeltine, I thank Jim Bean, Donna Brown, and Bill Wagner for their hours of conversations and clarifications. I also thank Jack Larsen for helping sponsor an in-house advanced Ada course on programming with APSE software tools. Finally, I thank Bill Griese, Ray Masak, Randy Cope, and Sal Nuzzo for their guidance and support.

> R. S. Freedman
> Huntington, NY 1985

SECTION ONE
INTRODUCTION AND OVERVIEW

1

What is
an APSE?

The purpose of an APSE (Ada Programming Support Environment) is to support the development and maintenance of Ada applications software throughout its life cycle, with particular emphasis on software for embedded computer applications."

This definition is from a document called Stoneman. Stoneman is a requirements document that defines an APSE in terms of the special needs associated with programming in the Ada language.

Experience has shown that there is more to programming than just knowing a language. We know that humans can be more productive if many functions connected with their work are automated. This is also true when humans are involved in building sophisticated computer programs. When the Ada language was being designed and specified (in conjunction with the language requirements documents called Woodenman, Tinman, Ironman, and finally Steelman), a parallel effort was also being investigated. This effort was concerned with defining the automated aids that would support Ada applications programming. The requirements for these automated aids went through a series of documents analogous to the language; in this case, the sets of requirements documents were called Sandman, Pebbleman, and finally, Stoneman. The resulting Stoneman document is thus the cornerstone to understanding and applying the Ada language to the development of real applications. The purpose of this section is to examine some of the Stoneman requirements and criteria. This is necessary in order to understand the principles behind an APSE.

We first start with trying to understand what Stoneman means by the "purpose of an APSE" in the above definition. We first observe that this definition is loaded with undefined terms: programming, environment, support, development, maintenance, Ada applications software, life cycle, embedded computer applications. Consequently, to fully understand what an APSE (rhymes with "caps") is supposed to be and how it may be used correctly, we will show what these terms mean. We first need a basic model for computation.

A programming language is a notation for specifying algorithms. A computer program is an algorithm that is specified in a programming language. We define software to be a collection of algorithms that is specified with a programming language.

There are advantages in using different notations for specifying different algorithms: we observe this frequently with mathematical notation. For example, mathematicians have provided us with different notations for specifying algorithms associated with rates of change (differential calculus) and for specifying algorithms associated with inference (predicate calculus). This has also been echoed in the programming language community: different programming languages have been defined to specify different classes of algorithms for different classes of applications. What makes the definition of programming languages challenging (as opposed to other formal notations used for specifying algorithms) is that the algorithm resulting from a programming language specification should be able to be carried out by a machine. At this point, the nature of the machine comes into question.

Computer scientists familiar with the theory of computation have developed a standard, abstact notion of a computer called a Turing Machine. Essentially, all one needs is a central processing unit with a small set of machine instructions and a transducer that enables data to be input and output from an external storage medium (with as much storage for input and output as one needs). This computer can then compute anything that is computable. All digital computers of the present (as well as those that will be built in the future) can be considered to be instances of this computer hardware. The differences between the Turing Machine and other computers are found in the physical limitations of real computers (Turing Machines have an infinite memory capacity as well as an infinite transducer access rate) and in the nature of the actual machine instructions (different machines may have different instruction sets in their central processor). This notion of a Turing machine is almost 50 years old.

Algorithms specified in a programming language based on a small set of machine instructions are all that one needs to prove theorems about computability. However, the specification of "practical" algorithms with a language similar to Turing machine instructions is usually very tedious for a human. It is more convenient (as well as more productive and economical) to develop a programming language that makes specifying algorithms easier for a human. Such a language is called a "high-level" language. If both the machine language and the higher-level language are formally specified, then we can routinely translate the high-level language into the machine language. The process by which an entire algorithm in one language is translated into a different language, such that the specifications represented in both languages have the same meaning, is called compilation. A compiler translates algorithms that are specified in a high-level programming language into a specification of machine instructions. (One goal of programming language design is to produce efficient automated compilers.)

We need one more definition to complete our basic computational model. When a specification of machine instructions is placed into this machine (possibly by some other machine instructions), and when some appropriate control instruction is given so that the machine is actually processing these instructions that denote the algorithm, then we say the software is "running" or "executing" on the machine. Sometimes this entire process is referred to as loading, invoking, and executing. We note that in this process the computer program (represented by a sequence of machine instructions) can be regarded as the input data to our machine. This process was also developed almost 50 years ago in the form of a "Universal Turing Machine."

This is our model of computation. There are some practical problems with this model. These problems are basically concerned with:

translating the algorithm into a programming language, and
translating the programming language into the machine instructions.

One practical concern deals with the mapping of meanings. Errors can occur when the human translates an algorithm into a representation in a programming language. This may happen if the human is not familiar with a particular programming language (or if he confuses it with another language). It may also happen if the original algorithm was flawed. Another practical concern deals with the wasted effort involved when humans translate the same algorithm into different programming languages.

One way around these practical difficulties is to follow what the computer theoreticians did 50 yeas ago. However, instead of standardizing a machine, we can standardize on a programming language. This is exactly what numerical analysts have done for the last 20 years: whenever a new numerical algorithm is reported in the literature, it is frequently specified in the programming language Algol 60. Having one language can make life easier for the human algorithm writer (since he only has one language to learn). Life is simpler for the human compiler writer as well: instead of having to write a compiler to translate every high-level language to every machine language (a many-to-many mapping), our labor is reduced by having to write a new compiler that translates our "standard" language to a new machine language (a one-to-many mapping). The amount of labor saved can be measured by splitting the compiler development into a "front-end" (reflecting machine independent algorithms) and a "back-end" (or "code generator" that isolates machine dependent algorithmic constructs). Having a standard language means that the effort of building a new compiler for a new machine is essentially equivalent to building a new code generator to an existing front-end. One important problem remains: validating the translations of meanings from the programming language to a machine language. This is sometimes called the compiler validation problem.

So far, what has been said can be applied to any programming language. Ada is a programming language that was designed especially for a certain area of application: the area of embedded computer systems. We now continue our investigation of the Stoneman definition of an APSE and apply our observations to the Ada world of embedded computers.

What is an embedded computer? According to Webster's Third New International Dictionary of the English Language (which forms part of the definition of the Ada language), something is embedded if it is "placed as to form an integral part of a whole." When a computer is (functionally) a minor (but important) part of a larger system (e.g., a control system, a communication switching system, a display, an avionics system), then we say that this computer is embedded in the system. The particular computer (and its associated peripherals), that is, part of the larger system, is called the embedded computer system.

In some ways, it is easier to see what an embedded computer system is not. It is not a system where the computer is the major functional part (as far as the entire system functionality is concerned). This usually includes large "time-shared" computers (used for "number-crunching" scientific calculation or accounting) and computer networks of these larger computers. If a computer is larger than a breadbox it typically is not an embedded computer.

Another characterization of these embedded computer systems is their responsiveness in a very "timely" matter. (This assumes that we can measure the responsiveness of the computer. To accomplish this, we would need to have a detailed knowledge of the implemented algorithm.) A computer where response time can be measured in hours and days before its "answer" to its "problem" can be given is typically not an embedded computer.

Embedded computer applications include sensor monitoring. Other applications may emphasize the control of equipment and displays. Still other applications may be where one needs a computer just to access, manipulate, and format data. What is common in these applications are the following:

1. The computer software will continue to execute in the presence of faults. This means that the specified algorithms have been designed to consider "exceptional situations."

2. Special peripheral devices (usually application specific, as opposed to "general purpose" devices) are available for communication with the computer.

3. Special requests to the processor from these devices (sometimes called interrupts) can be handled in "real-time" (in other words, quickly).

Another important term in the Stoneman definition of an APSE was that of "life-cycle." Any large, complex system frequently seems to take a life unto itself. This includes large software systems. The birth and death cycle usually appears like this:

7

```
loop
    define the problem
    formulate the requirements
    specify the approach to the solution
    design the solution
    implement what was designed
    validate what was done
    maintain the implementation (in old age), which involves
        identifying new problems
    exit when retired
end loop
```

This cycle is well known in software engineering. It shows the typical evolution of any complex system. Complex jobs should be initially well formulated with detailed sets of definitions, requirements, and constraints. The next steps reflect an attempt at a solution, where an approach is identified, designed, and carried out. We then make sure that our solution really is the solution to the problem that was given to us: this is the purpose of the validation steps. Finally, after the development job is done, someone must still be around to answer questions that surface in the actual application environment, and to be around to fix things that may go wrong. One may expect that if the solution was carefully designed to fit the problem, then this maintenance step would be fairly routine. Unfortunately, in real life, this maintenance step is frequently the most aggravating and most expensive. This reflects poor discipline in designing the solution to our problem.

Strictly speaking, there really is not one cycle (loop) in this model: after every step there should be a retrospective cycle. This retrospective miniloop process that occurs after each lifecycle step is called verification. Verification is part of an overall strategy (called quality assurance) that insures a quality deliverable product.

Most applications do not last forever. There must be an established criteria for terminating the project (usually by replacing it by another one). This is indicated by the retired switch in the exit statement of the above loop. This termination may also be part of an overall strategy called configuration management.

The word "support" in the Stoneman definition of an APSE refers to the support of efforts that primarily involves a lot of thinking, writing, and trying out of ideas. In normal "office work" this is frequently supported by file cabinets and secretaries who serve as translators, editors, word and text processors, letter openers for mail and other correspondance, and meeting schedulers. We note that some offices provide better support (and hence, better working environments) than other offices. In the Ada world, work is much more specialized and a different set of requirements for Ada work exist than for "normal" business work. However, the same analogy holds for Ada work: life is made easier when one has a good Ada Programming Support Environment.

When one is supporting the "old age" of a system (i.e., maintenance), there are several components that one would wish to have at his fingertips. This is reminiscent of a doctor treating his patients. Part of this documentation includes the date and purpose of each visit, what was diagnosed, what was prescribed, and when the next visit would be. Also included would be billing information, data on which insurance forms were filled out, and so on. This information is necessary for the doctor if he wants to manage and control his business. The doctor needs to keep his patients healthy and happy: if he makes too many errors on either a technical (medical) or management (paperwork) level, he will lose his patients.

Most business organizations as part of their normal work routine include records of why decisions were made, records of system variations and revisions, and records of bills. Many of these records are kept confidential. In the Ada world similar records are kept: this is all part of configuration management.

In summary, the Ada language supports the development of algorithms for embedded computer systems. The APSE supports the life cycle deployment of Ada application software.

We also make one further note that reveals a tradition for automated software life cycle support. We call the embedded computer for which our Ada software is written the "target computer." We also have automated aids that support our Ada software development: it should be noted that these automated aids must also reside on a computer. The computer that holds all our automated Ada life cycle support for our application is called the host computer. The APSE essentially assumes this distributed model of software development.

References

The basic reference for the definition of an APSE is found in Stoneman [17]. The Turing Machine is described in [52] and in most books on the theory of computation; a good reference is [16]. Many of our ideas on the software life cycle are found in [11], [21], and [33]. A good general bibliography of Ada-related references is [45].

Problems

1. Give some examples of programming languages that were developed to easily specify algorithms in (a) arithmetic, (b) string manipulation, (c) symbol manipulation.

2. Show how a compiler can compile itself.

3. Give examples of embedded computer systems that can be found in the home, in the office, in a car, and where one might least suspect to find one.

4. What records should be kept confidential between managers, customers, and programmers in developing a large Ada application?

2

Why Do We Need an APSE?

We will answer the question posed by the title of this chapter after we first examine exactly what Ada (as defined in [1], also known as the Ada Reference Manual, Ada RM, Ada Language Reference Manual, or LRM) provides and leaves out.

First, what makes Ada, Ada? Ada consists of programming structures:

packages.
subprograms,
generic packages
generic subprograms.

An Ada package is the basic unit of modularity. Packages separate declarative specifications of algorithms (the specification part) from procedural specification of algorithms (the body part). The package specification forms the interface or contract between the writer of the package and the user. Packages are the chief vehicle for information hiding. Packages are built from subprograms, Ada objects and types, and other packages.

Ada subprograms encapsulate our notion of a command. Subprograms are the chief carriers of procedural information associated with an algorithm.

Generic packages and generic subprograms further abstract the properties of packages and subprograms by allowing the creation of templates of packages and templates of subprograms. These templates can be "instantiated" into concrete packages and programs. The Ada predefined packages for input and output of "generic" items are specified in terms of generic packages.

All of these structures help an Ada programmer think in terms of software components that may be separately designed, developed, and compiled. We also recall that these compiled structures inhabit what the RM calls a program library.

Finally, the Ada programming structures provide important life cycle support to an application during the design and maintenance stages. During these stages, modularity and organization are crucial aids in determining if a component works or not. A bad software component should be replaceable without affecting the rest of the application.

Ada consists of data structures. These structures specify the following data types (with an associated set of predefined operations):

> enumeration types,
> real types (fixed and floating point),
> record types,
> integer types,
> array types,
> access types,
> derived types,
> Boolean types
> character types,
> string types,
> private types.

Ada objects (variables) can be declared to belong to one of these types. This enables the construction of entities having a certain structure and having a certain set of allowable predefined operations that may manipulate these entities. These data structures also make an Ada programmer think abstractly, so that unnecessary information about a particular data structure can be hidden.

Finally, Ada consists of tasks. Tasks enable Ada to be a convenient notation for specifying algorithms involving concurrent processes. Tasks can also be templated (abstracted into a data structure) with the task type mechanism.

As with other languages, Ada is specified by its syntax and its semantics. The syntax of a language can also be decomposed into the abstract syntax and the concrete syntax. The concrete syntax of Ada is, shown in Appendix E of the RM. This shows the rules by which "well-formed" Ada programs can be written. The abstract syntax of Ada consists of the Ada constructs that are assigned a meaning. This syntax is also presented (informally) in the LRM. One formal notation that is used for specifying the abstract syntax of Ada is called Diana. Diana is an acronym that stands for Descriptive Intermediate Attributed Notation for Ada.

The semantics of a language is the specification of meaning associated with the language. One way of specifying the semantics of a language is to use the abstract syntax as a guide and to specify meanings of a construct in terms of the meanings of its subconstructs. This is called the denotational approach to semantics. Another way of specifying semantics is to construct a "virtual machine" and define the meanings of the language constructs in terms of the execution of these constructs on the virtual machine. This is the operational approach to semantics. The semantics of Ada are described somewhat differently in the RM. In the RM, Ada is specified "by means of narrative rules." Formal and technical terms that are not defined with these rules in the RM are assumed to be defined in Webster's Third International Dictionary of the English Language. Another guide to the semantics of Ada is contained in the Ada Compiler Implementer's Validation Guide, and in the Ada compiler test suite.

What the RM expressly leaves out are pragmatics. Pragmatics are associated with any language and specifies the culture or "folklore" of that language. One obvious pragmatic is concerned with the maximum number of dimensions for an array. Another pragmatic can simply be the length of an identifier. Different compiler implementations may allow for different lengths. These are not specified in the RM because to do so may bias Ada compiler builders to certain machine technologies.

There are other important concepts and mechanisms that the RM does not explicitly define. One reason is that they do not have anything to do with specifying a language. However, clarifying these "undefinitions" are necessary in order to use Ada on a real machine. Some of these undefinitions are spelled out in the RM; we summarize them below.

The RM does not define the mechanism whereby an Ada program unit is compiled, executed, or controlled. This is not a language issue. Having different mechanisms for these functions may defeat one of the purposes behind a common standard language. Programs may still have to be reinvented to conform to particular implementations.

The RM does not specify the size or speed of execution of a particular construct. This is a pragmatic issue that, if specified, can impact the decision of machine implementation.

The RM does not define the form or content of listings, warnings, or messages. This is also a pragmatic concern. Humans do not necessarily want formally specified messages. Some may want more information, and some may want less.

The RM does not define the semantics associated with executing a particular construct that contains a violation that a validated Ada compiler is not required to detect. This protects the compiler validation suite. No one can guarantee what can happen if an unforseen implementation quirk (that the compiler validation suite does not catch) exists in some implementation.

The RM does not define the size of program units that may exceed the capacity of a target machine. This is another machine technological pragmatic.

Naturally, these items must be defined somewhere for some real implementation! Other Ada undefinitions are more subtle.

The Ada RM does not define what causes the end of a line. Why is this important? One reason is that the size of Ada identifiers depend on the size of a line.

The RM defines a main program in terms of the structure of a subprogram that is a library unit. The RM further specifies that the execution of the main program acts as if it were called by some "environment task." The issue of main programs having parameters is not defined. This is important when one considers the mechanisms of how programs are invoked.

The RM defines a program library as an entity that contains the compilation units of a compilation. Can there be more than one program library? What are the commands for creating program libraries? How do we check the status of a program library? The RM indicates that a solution should exist but recognizes that such a solution does not belong in a language specification. The Ada program library is one of the most important features of the language that can impact an application during the design and maintenance stages of its life cycle. The mechanisms governing the use of the library must be specified in order to provide separate compilation and software component development. Suitable specification of this mechanism can also lead to the sharing of program libraries.

The RM specifies that if a main program has tasks, then the main program terminates when these tasks (and all other dependent tasks) terminate. Suppose a main program uses a library package which in turn has dependent tasks. The RM says that the main program does not await the termination of those tasks. The question is, what happens to those tasks? One may want to have some mechanism to kill them after the main program finishes; otherwise they may waste precious computer resources. This mechanism is not specified in the language.

The RM defines input and output of variables to and from the external program environment in terms of several predefined packages. External files are identified to the Ada program with the help of two parameters, NAME and FORM. Both are strings. The RM does not define how these strings are interpreted (of course it is up to the implementation). If programs are to be shared, then the use of these file names must be carefully specified.

There are several Ada language constructs whose meanings are specified only in the context of a particular implementation. These constructs include:

pragmas,
attributes,
exceptions,
representation clauses,
system dependent names,
machine code insertions.

Pragmas pass certain information to the Ada compiler. The predefined pragmas that deal with the details associated with storage are:

15

CONTROLLED

MEMORY_SIZE

OPTIMIZE

PACK

SHARED

STORAGE_UNIT

Two of these, MEMORY_SIZE and STORAGE_UNIT, act like assignments: they can tell a compiler to compile a particular program with those particular memory units. Here is an example showing the effect that an implementation has on the meaning of the pragma:

pragma MEMORY_SIZE (13);

with MY_IO; with SYSTEM;

procedure Mainl is

  -- definitions , actions

  --

    if SYSTEM.MEMORY_SIZE < 12 then DoSomething;

  --

  end Mainl;

  -- The pragma has the effect of changing MEMORY_SIZE.
  -- The meaning of the program then depends on this imple-
  -- mentation dependency.

The predefined pragmas that deal with names and binding are:

INTERFACE

ELABORATE

SYSTEM_NAME

SYSTEM_NAME also acts like an assignment; in this case, the name of the target system can be provided to the compiler. INTERFACE provides an Ada compiler with a mechanism for using programs specified in another language. The exact mechanism for using non-Ada programs is not specified in the RM. Here is an example using INTERFACE:

```
package UseFortran is

    function ATAN(X:Float)return Float;

private

    pragma INTERFACE(Fortran,ATAN);

end;

--   The meaning of the Ada function ATAN is reduced to the meaning
--   of Fortran function ATAN. If this package is to be shared, it is im-
--   portant to specify which Fortran dialect is intended
```

The pragmas that deal with timing and control are:

OPTIMIZE

INLINE

SUPPRESS

PRIORITY

One problem with pragma PRIORITY is that it may be implemented in several different ways, depending on whether an implementation schedules tasks or interrupts tasks. Pragma OPTIMIZE also depends on an implementation. An Ada program that was not compiled with the OPTIMIZE pragma may not be (pragmatically) feasible for a particular application.

All of the above pragmas primarily effect the implementation steps in the application life cycle. The remaining two pragmas, LIST and PAGE, exist for the enlightenment of the human reader of listings (which we observed above has no predefined form or meaning according to the RM). These two pragmas are useful throughout the life cycle to aid in document preparation.

Attributes represent certain "basic" operations or entities. The attributes that are concerned with storage details are:

ADDRESS

SIZE

STORAGE_SIZE

These attributes may be interrogated in an Ada program. Here is an example with ADDRESS:

```
procedure Main3 is

    X: NATURAL := 3;

begin

   << loop >>

        if <<loop>>'ADDRESS >32 then

            X:= 4;

            goto <<out>>;

        end if;

   <<out>> null;

    end Main3;

--   The meaning of the procedure depends on the way the implemen-
--   tation orders storage units.
```

There are several attributes that deal with naming and binding. They are associated with the different representations of types:

Scalar types: FIRST

                 LAST

Discrete types: WIDTH

POS

VAL

SUCC

PRED

IMAGE

VALUE

Floating point: DIGITS

MANTISSA

EPSILON

EMAX

SMALL

LARGE

SAFE_SMALL

SAFE_EMAX

SAFE_LARGE

MACHINE_RADIX

MACHINE_MANTISSA

MACHINE_EMAX

MACHINE_EMIN

MACHINE_ROUNDS

MACHINE_OVERFLOWS

Fixed point: DELTA

                    MANTISSA

                    SMALL

                    LARGE

                    FORE

                    AFT

                    MACHINE_ROUNDS

                    MACHINE_OVERFLOWS

The RM warns (Section 13.7.3) that programs that use the above attributes prefixed by MACHINE_ go beyond the properties associated with the Ada model numbers. "Precautions must therefore be taken when using these machine-dependent attributes if portability is to be ensured." Here is an example with MACHINE_OVERFLOWS:

```
with MyIO; use MyIO;

procedure Main4 is

    X,Y: Float := 10.0e02;

begin

    if Float'MACHINE_OVERFLOWS then

        Y: = X*X;

    end if;

exception

    when NUMERIC_ERROR = > put ("correctly handled");

end;
```

-- According to the RM, Section 4.5.7, an implementation is not re-
-- quired to detect an overflow. This program is implementation
-- dependent.

Array type: FIRST

FIRST(N)

LAST

LAST(N)

RANGE

RANGE(N)

LENGTH

LENGTH(N)

record types: CONSTRAINED (for private types)

FIRST_BIT

LAST_BIT

POSITION

Like address and size, the last three can be interrogated and provide information on details associated with the particular implementation. Here is an example:

```
with MyIO;

procedure Main5 is

    type Fraction is

        record

            NUM: Integer;
```

```
                DEN: Integer;

            end record;

        X,Y,Z: Fraction : = Fraction'(NUM = >1, DEN = >3);

    begin

            if Z.NUM'LAST_BIT > 32 then

                X.NUM : = Y.DEN'POSITION;

            end if;

    end;
```

-- The meaning of the program depends on how record storage units
-- are managed.

All types: BASE

Attributes that deal with timing and control are:

CALLABLE

COUNT

TERMINATED

The actual use of some of these attributes may give different program results for different target computers. Since some of these attributes refer to characteristics of some machine, the actual meaning of just what these attributes denote depends on the context of an implementation. All of the attributes predefined only effect the implementation stage in the application life cycle. We did not discuss here other pragmas and attributes that are not predefined: the effects of these are deferred to Appendix F of the RM.

Exceptions are the Ada way of dealing with situations that do not arise during normal program execution, but which can be anticipated by a programmer. The Ada predefined exceptions are raised during certain anticipated situations that may occur. It may be possible to raise these exceptions on one implementation, while on another implementation, execution may be considered "normal." The exception that is raised when a storage inconsistency is apparent is called STORAGE_ERROR. This exception is raised if, during program execution, allocated storage runs out. Two exceptions are concerned when naming and binding inconsistencies arise. They are CONSTRAINT_ERROR and NUMERIC_ERROR. Finally, the exceptions that deal with control are called PROGRAM_ERROR and TASKING_ERROR. PROGRAM_ERROR is raised when "erroneous" behavior is recognized. These exceptions affect the implementation stages of the application life cycle. Here is an example showing that raising an exception may depend on the implementation:

```
procedure Main6;

    X,Y: Float : =  1.0e6;

begin

    X : =  X**X;

exception

    when NUMERIC_ERROR  = > DoSomething;

    when others  = > DoSomeThingElse;

end;
```

```
--   The question is, what exception will be raised?
--   (An implementation is not required to raise NUMERIC_ERROR
--   in overflow situations.)
```

A representation clause is another Ada mechanism that specifies how Ada types can be represented by machine structures. Addresses, lengths, and alignments can be specified. Enumeration types can also be "encoded" to a specific machine.

As documented in Appendix F of the RM, an implementation must specify several characteristics (some of which were outlined above). A very important specification concerns the nature of the names in package SYSTEM. The entire package is implementation dependent: using anything that depends on this package is not defined in the Ada language simply because it is left to the implementation to define.

Further details on implementation dependent features and representation clauses are discussed in Chapter 13 of the Ada RM. One feature not discussed there (but mentioned in Section 14) is the nature of file-naming for input and output. File naming conventions on different machines are not necessarily the same. A program may not be able to be shared if it depends on certain file names. So—

```
with Text_IO

procedure Main7 is

    MyFile:File_Type;

begin

    Create (MyFile, "RSF:MAIN_9.ADA");

    Put (MyFile, "This Works");

end;

--   This may not work if the file system of the host computer
--   has file names that look like this: <RSF> MAIN_9'(ADA)
```

File naming is not the only aspect of input and output that depends on an implementation. The RM does not specify whether a file is or is not closed by the implementation when a program that opens a file terminates.

The last category of features that the Ada language allows—but which leaves the semantics to the implementation—are machine code insertions. Obviously, any Ada program that uses machine code insertions has its semantics defined in terms of the particular machine code instructions. According to the RM, an implementation must define a package called MACHINE_CODE (for the particular machine) which specifies the actual machine instructions in terms of an Ada record syntax structure. As an example, we specify the package TURING_MACHINE_CODE that shows how some Turing machine instructions may be specified:

```
package TURING_MACHINE_CODE is

    type OPERATOR is (STO,ADD,BRA);
```

-- STOre accumulator contents at address.

-- ADD contents of address to accumulator.

-- BRAnch to address if accumulator contents are zero.

type OPERAND is NATURAL;

type TURING is

record

OP1 : OPERATOR;

OP2 : OPERAND

end record;

end TURING_MACHINE_CODE;

We create a machine dependent program made up of Ada allowable machine code statements. Again, just because the Ada R M defines this construct, it does not mean that we can assign meaning to a program that utilizes this construct. The semantics of these programs depends on the semantics of the machine, not on anything defined in the R M.

with TURING_MACHINE_CODE;

procedure GUESS is

use TURING_MACHINE_CODE;

begin

TURING'(OP1 = >ADD,OP2 = >1);

TURING'(OP1 = >STO,OP2 = >3);

TURING'(OP1 = >ADD,OP2 = >2);

TURING'(OP1 = >STO,OP2 = >1);

TURING'(OP1 = >ADD,OP2 = >3);

```
        TURING'(OP1 = >STO,OP2 = >2);

    end GUESS;
```

In summary, Ada is a notation. A notation should be sufficient to specify a design for a particular application, but is not enough to make that application real by magically turning it into machine instructions. Even though the ADA RM defines very many characteristics that are important for implementing algorithms for embedded computer applications, many other characteristics are either defined in terms of a particular target machine or are not defined at all. In addition, outside of the Ada library, separate compilation facilities and certain pragma listing aids, there is no adequate support for Ada applications throughout the application life cycle that is specified by the language. Consequently, to use Ada reliably and efficiently, we need an APSE.

The next chapter observes what requirements an APSE should satisfy.

References

An informal introduction to the semantics of Ada is found in [26]. Good introductions to programming language semantics are found in [49] and [51]. Ada semantics is described more formally in [2] and [36] and in the Ada compiler implementor's guide [28]. The Diana Reference Guide [29] provides more information on the details associated with Diana. The effects of Ada pragmatics on Ada programs are discussed in [55].

Problems

1. One Ada controversy is concerned with creating an Ada "subset." Show that, pragmatically, most Ada programs are written in a subset of the Ada language.

2. Many are heard to complain that Ada is "too large." Interpret this statement with respect to syntax, semantics, and pragmatics.

3. Give an example of a main program that uses a package that has dependent tasks.

4. Give an example of some Ada programs that may not be shared between targets or hosts by including in the definition of these programs (a) pragmas, (b) attributes, or (c) exceptions.

3

What are the Requirements for an APSE?

It is no coincidence that the development of the requirements for the Ada programming language (Steelman) proceeded in parallel with the development of the requirements for a programming support environment that would support that language. In those unromantic days when Ada was known as DOD-1, it was realized that the chief benefit of a "common standard" language would not be realized unless there were adequate support facilities: otherwise, DOD-1 would end up being another COBOL, FORTRAN, or JOVIAL. About six months before Ada was born in the preliminary July standard, the set of requirements for Ada Programming Support Environments known as Stoneman was published. When we refer to an APSE, we refer to an APSE as specified in Stoneman.

There are other analogies between the development of the Ada language and the development of the Ada Programming Support Environment. It has been said that the Ada language is not a revolutionary development in language design; Ada represents a consolidation of several good ideas found in many programming languages. In fact, the LRM tells us that the Ada designers were influenced by the concepts found in the languages Pascal, Simula, CLU, Euclid, and Mesa. Many people learning Ada for the first time tell us that Ada "looks" like Pasal or PL/I (usually depending on which language they learned first). This informal observation of concrete syntax and semantics reflects the intentions of the Steelman language requirements: Ada should incorporate the modern principles of software engineering (as exemplified in several modern languages) but still be easy to learn.

The APSE is also not a revolutionary development in programming support environments. It similarly represents a consolidation of several good ideas found in other programming support environments. Many of the concepts associated with an APSE can be traced to the support environments found in several modern operating systems. These operating systems provide programming support that is based on many principles of software engineering. One important principle is that useful computer programs that help build other computer programs ("software tools" or "utilities") can be shared. A dual principle is similar to the concept of "information hiding" in programming languages: access to programs (or any other stored information) should be controlled.

Other good ideas that are reflected in the APSE are concerned with uniform, integrated support for one language concentrating on one application domain. Stoneman acknowledges the Interlisp programming support environment for these ideas. The Interlisp programming support environment consists of a uniform set of "software tools" that supports the development of artificial intelligence applications. The applications programs are written in Lisp, and the programming support environment is also written in Lisp. This encourages sharing of tools and applications programs. Since all work is done in Lisp, humans do not have to go through extensive retraining when they move to another host machine having the Interlisp environment. These ideas are incorporated in the APSE since it is required that applications programs and the programming support resources both be written in Ada.

We now consider the Stoneman components of an APSE. An APSE is a software system that consists of the following three main components:

a data base;
an interface between a human APSE user and the

APSE software as well as an interface between the different
APSE software components;
a toolset.

These components share the common goal of promoting the sharing
of user programs and tools.

The data base is the central repository for information associated with each Ada application. This information is stored throughout the life cycle of the application.

The interface controls the data base and also controls the use
of tools. Associated with the human interface is a special language
that enables actions to be performed or certain expressions to be
evaluated on command of the human. This interface is sometimes
called a "job control language" (or simply just a "control language"), a "command language," or a "monitor language."

The toolset contains tools (sometimes called "software tools").
These tools are the automated aids for program development, maintenance, quality assurance, and configuration management that are
to be used throughout the life cycle of the application.

One natural question to ask is, "What is meant by sharing?"
There are three levels of sharing, corresponding to the concerns of
the tool, the human APSE user, and the Ada application.

We would like a tool to be shared among different APSE users.
If this tool proves to be very popular, we would like to use this tool
on any APSE installation. Are we able to share tools between APSEs?
We can if we can figure out a mechanism that enables us to "move"
a particular tool from one APSE to another. This sharing problem is
sometimes referred to as tool portability. A tool is portable if the
cost of moving this tool from one APSE to another (either on the
same or on a different computer) is as little as possible.

Another type of sharing is seen in many (human) management
situations. In many organizations, we would like our workers to be
able to work on different projects (at possibly different sites). In the
Ada world, this corresponds to having APSE users work on different
applications using possibly different APSEs. In this case, we are not
sharing APSE tools or APSE resources: our intention is to share human resources. User portability is when human APSE users are able
to move from one project to another (or from one APSE to another)
without extensive retraining. This can be reasonably accomplished
if the human interfaces on the different APSEs are similar.

Sometimes we not only want to share tools and humans, we

also want to share the actual application program as well. This is an issue of project portability. This refers to the cost of moving an entire project and all its support tools and application-specific programs between host computers. This can happen several times during a project life cycle, especially if different computers are used during different stages. It may happen that one host is used for requirements generation, another for documentation, and yet another for detailed documentation.

There is a degree of overlap between all these notions of sharing. The question that remains is: What kind of support model should we require that can support all these levels of sharing?

The model that Stoneman recommends to achieve these levels of portability was used before, but in a completely different context. The model suggested is reminiscent of the model of layered communication network protocols that has been specified by the International Standards Organization (ISO). The basic idea is to hide unnecessary detail from a user or controller of resources. This model is very typical of any complex organizational hierarchy, as found in armies, schools, or corporations.

For example, a typical military hierarchy is shown in Figure 3.1. The highest level of control is denoted by the general. The general makes the highest level decisions to get a job done. His requests are served by his colonels. The colonels similarly control the majors, and majors order captains. Finally, on the lowest level, the privates are the basic resource to accomplish an objective. We note that generals talk to generals: the communications link between officers on the same level is called a protocol. Generals rarely talk to sergeants or corporals: this would be a violation of protocol. Generals give orders to colonels: the communications link between officers and their immediate inferiors (or superiors) is called an interface. The interesting thing about these orders is that the superior officer is often not concerned with the details of the implementation of his orders.

Figure 3.2 shows the ISO model of communication protocols. This model is also called OSI, for Open System Interconnection. The ISO model is primarily concerned with the links between communication devices. Like the military case, these links are either protocols or interfaces. The common theme between these examples is that higher levels control the resources available to lower levels. This control is disciplined by a strict set of interfaces. Protocols establish relations between the resources of different instantiations of

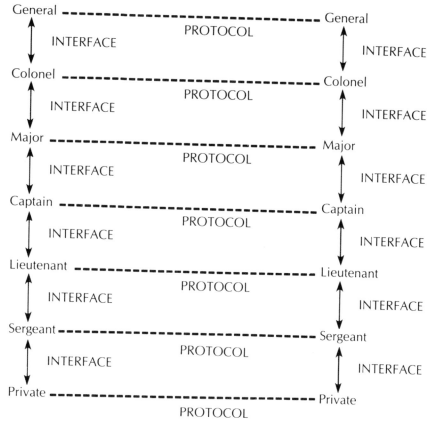

Figure 3.1. Protocols and interfaces (military).

a generic entity (like two colonels), provided that these resources are on the same level.

The APSE model is shown in Figure 3.3. In the APSE, the lowest level of resources corresponds to the actual operating system of whatever host computer we happen to be on. The next level of resources is called a KAPSE, or Kernel Ada Programming Support Environment. It is the KAPSE that controls the resources of the host computer in this model. The next level up in abstraction is called a MAPSE, or Minimal Ada Programming Support Environment. This layer contains the set of tools that are used throughout the life cycle of an Ada project. These tools exploit the resources of the host computer "through" the KAPSE; in this sense, it is said that the KAPSE represents a "machine independent interface," or a "virtual Ada machine." Just as a general controls his army through his lieu-

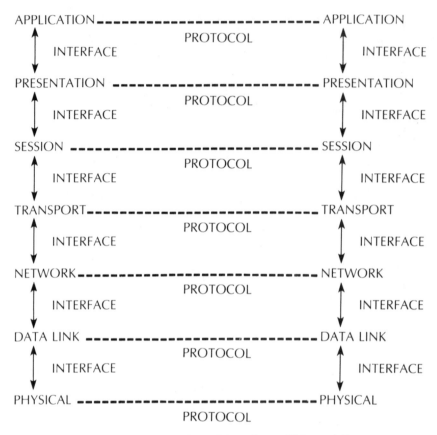

Figure 3.2 Protocols and interfaces (ISO model).

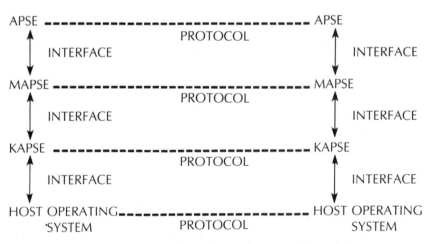

Figure 3.3. Protocols and interfaces (APSE model).

tenants, the MAPSE controls the host machine resources through the KAPSE. By an abuse of language, an APSE can refer to this entire model, or it can refer to levels higher than the MAPSE level.

There is a strategy that Stoneman observes that shows how to achieve MAPSE-level resource sharing between two hosts, each with its own APSE:

1. Build the MAPSE in Ada.

2. Isolate machine and host operating system dependencies of these MAPSE resources to the KAPSE.

3. Sharing the MAPSE resources on another host (a MAPSE-to-MAPSE protocol) is accomplished by recompiling the MAPSE resources with the host Ada compiler.

The trick here is to make sure that the MAPSE-to-KAPSE interfaces are the same on both APSEs. We will examine the issues involved with this specification in a later chapter. If there is no APSE (or KAPSE) on the other host, we can still share our MAPSE resources on the other host, but more work is required. We replace step 3 with:

3.1. Build a new KAPSE for the other host; build an Ada compiler for the new host (a host operating system interface).

3.2. Recompile the MAPSE resources.

We thus further specify who is who in the APSE world.

The APSE user builds applications. He needs all the help he can get in developing and maintaining his Ada programs and delivering them to his customer.

The MAPSE user also builds applications, though some of his applications may consist in building special purpose APSE tools (that may be built from other MAPSE tools). At this point, we make the following observation: the only difference between a MAPSE toolset and an APSE toolset is that an APSE toolset is meant to be extensible, and the MAPSE toolset represents the smallest toolset you should use to develop any worthwhile Ada application. What does this minimal toolset include? As far as supporting the Ada language is concerned, we need a compiler and a library tool (for separate compilation support), and a linker (for creating "main" programs). Other necessary tools are discussed in the next and later chapters.

A KAPSE user is concerned with building tools, especially MAPSE tools. Since the KAPSE controls the machine resources, it is directly responsible for keeping track of storage details and for the mechanisms by which tools are invoked. All MAPSE and APSE users may use the KAPSE directly or indirectly.

We now focus on the actual KAPSE interfaces. There are really two: one between the KAPSE and MAPSE and one between the KAPSE and the host operating system. We want to make these interfaces explicit so we can understand their use to APSE tool users and tool builders.

Both KAPSE interfaces can be informally specified with the semantics of Ada. The KAPSE controls the actual machine resources; part of the KAPSE must therefore be implemented in a host dependent language (possibly host machine language). The interface between the KAPSE and the host operating system can be described with the following Ada package:

```
package KAPSE_OS_INTERFACE is

    --   Specifications of Ada program entities

    --   that may help describe the host

    --   operating system primitives, like
         procedure BIND_FILE_NAME;


    --                        •

    --   and so on.



end KAPSE__OS_INTERFACE:
```

```
--   This package specification is the operating system interface
--   used by KAPSE builders. The actual host operating system
--   primitives are implemented in the package body:


with HOST_MACHINE_CODE;
```

package body KAPSE_OS_INTERFACE is

    --   The implementation of operating system
    --   interfaces in the host machine language, e.g.

    procedure BIND_FILE_NAME is

        --   would contain machine code statements, like

        MY_HOST'(Operator1 = >STO,
                    Operator2 = >33);
        --   and so on.

    end BIND_FILE_NAME;

end KAPSE_OS_INTERFACE;

The KAPSE-MAPSE interfaces can be similarly described in terms of Ada package semantics. For example, a KAPSE package that supports some input-output services may be specified by:

    package MAPSE_KAPSE_IO _INTERFACE is

        --   This package is used by the MAPSE and APSE
        --   tools that request input-output services from the
        --   host (and can only be obtained through the
        --   KAPSE).
        --   One example procedure is

        procedure DEFAULT_FILE_NAME(X:out STRING);

    end MAPSE_KAPSE_IO_INTERFACE;

--   This package specification is the KAPSE interface used
--   by MAPSE tool builders. The actual KAPSE primitives
--   are implemented in the package body;

    with KAPSE_OS;

35

```
package body MAPSE_KAPSE_IO_INTERFACE is

--   The implementation of the
--   calls to the KAPSE.

    procedure DEFAULT_FILE_NAME(X:out NAME;
    . . .) is

        --   The implementation of the service containing
        --   host dependent operations, like

    KAPSE_OS.BIND_FILE_ NAME;

        --   Note how the implementation is hidden from
        --   the tool builder.

    end DEFAULT_FILE_NAME;

end MAPSE_KAPSE_IO_INTERFACE;
```

These MAPSE-KAPSE interfaces are an important area of the APSE world because they govern tool sharing between KAPSEs. In fact, we will see later that one may characterize an APSE by its KAPSE! And, more important, standardizing the MAPSE-KAPSE interfaces essentially is standardizing a KAPSE. This effort is being aided by two groups: the KIT and the KITIA. These acronyms stand for KAPSE Interface Team and Kapse Interface Team Industry and Academia.

We will now examine some refinements of the concept of sharing. The next several definitions are seen throughout the Ada and APSE worlds.

Transportability is the degree to which an APSE tool can be installed on a different APSE without reprogramming. When the tool executes on the other APSE, its behavior (functionality) must be the same.

Interoperability is the degree to which an APSE can change data base objects (and the relationships between those objects) without reprogramming. The exchanged objects must be usable on the other APSE.

Reusability is the degree to which one can actually use an Ada program unit (without reprogramming) in the construction of new Ada programs.

A host is a computer system that has an APSE. The APSE supports Ada software development and maintenance. The APSE tools execute (run) on the host.

A target is a computer system that executes Ada programs. This is somewhat tricky. A host is a target because APSE tools are written in Ada. A target may or may not be a host. An embedded target is used for embedded computer applications. One interesting problem is in considering what KAPSE support is required for targets.

Rehostability is the degree to which an APSE can be installed on a different host with needed reprogramming localized to the KAPSE.

Retargetability is the degree to which an Ada program does not have to be modified to accomplish the same function with respect to another target.

References

Stoneman [17] specifies the APSE model. Further information on the OSI model is found in [12] and [37]. The correspondence between the OSI model and the APSE is discussed in [35]. An APSE model of the services of the VMS operating system is in [34]. An analysis of KAPSE interfaces of different APSES is given in [23]. Activities of the KIT and KITIA are documented in the Public Reports, [43] and [44]. The Interlisp environment is documented in [50].

Problems

1. "Writing programs in Ada will enable all programs to be shared among any computers with an Ada compiler." Criticize this statement.

2. Will an Ada program that uses the KAPSE interfaces instead of directly communicating with the operating system always be sharable? What about pragmatics?

3. Does retargetability imply rehostability? Does rehostability imply retargetability? Illustrate with examples.

4. Is a host computer specified only by its "hardware" (machine language instruction set, also sometimes called instruction set architecture), or by its software (operating system or "resident" programming support environment). Discuss the purposes of each specification.

4

APSE
Components

We have previously observed that an APSE consists of a data base, a set of tools, and an interface that glues the entire assembly to make an integrated system. We now focus on the two crucial APSE components—the data base and the toolset—to see what makes them unique.

These two APSE components reflect the immediate concern of the Ada programmer: life cycle Ada support for his application. Again, we emphasize two facts which are perhaps fairly obvious:

1. The APSE provides support facilities (as opposed to no support facilities).

2. The support facilities that the APSE provides are special purpose (as opposed to general purpose).

It is helpful to see what this means in another application domain, so we introduce the cooking paradigm. It is very difficult (a bit primitive, but not impossible) to bake bread using general purpose tools like a hammer or a ruler. In fact, one might say that the quality, reliability, and efficiency of baking bread without any support tools leaves much to be desired.

Baking bread in a kitchen is a different story. We have tools that help us prepare and tools that help us implement what we have prepared (an oven). We also have access to documentation, so that the results of our cooking experiences can be recorded (in a recipe book). So, the quality of our product improves. However, the reliability of our product is not as high as the reliability that one expects from a professional baker. The professional bread baker has an integrated set of very special purpose tools that support the entire life cycle of bread making, from purchasing the right amount of flour to packaging and boxing the product for the customer. The professional baker also has to be prepared for situations that arise when the customer is unsatisfied. This dissatisfaction may be due to management difficulties (i.e., late or incorrect deliveries) or due to technical difficulties (i.e., a bug was caught in the flour and was delivered in a baked loaf). If a recipe or tool was inappropriately used he must isolate the cause and quickly correct the action. The professional bread baker knows that his tools are optimized for his application. His procedures are carefully managed and controlled; some of these procedures may be secret recipes or legally protected by copyright or trademark. He knows that he can produce an entire variety of products, and that his customers will be happy because they are getting the best product at lowest cost (otherwise, he would be out of business). The professional bread baker also knows that a good deal of training and apprenticeship in learning how to use his tools of the trade was part of his professional education.

The professional bread baker interacts not only with his customers but also with other professional bakers (cookie bakers, cake bakers, bagel bakers). All these professionals have similar concerns, although each professional has his own distinct set of support facilities. All these professionals also know that their jobs would be very hard to do (and their products would indeed suffer) if they worked in a general purpose environment, or if they worked in an environment with only one support tool.

This is all very similar in the Ada world. (In fact, since bread is usually an important part of a meal, but certainly not the purpose of a meal, we can consider the bread served at a table to be food that is "embedded" into a meal, in much the same way that an Ada target can be "embedded" into an application system.) The APSE user knows that his environment is optimized for his application. He knows that the tools of his trade are designed for the economical development and support of reliable, high-quality Ada software. The APSE user can produce an entire range of useful Ada applications, and his customer knows that these applications are cost-effective and the best that he could buy. The APSE user interacts with other system engineers (digital designers, numerical analysts, communication network specialists). Each one has his own specific toolset. The APSE user also knows that his product would suffer if he used a "general-purpose" toolset, or if he only used one important tool (like a compiler).

The APSE user knows that his APSE components allow him to do several useful and versatile functions.

The APSE user can create data base objects. These objects can contain specifications, designs, documentation and testing suites for the quality assurance of an application. The data base objects may also contain the application program written in Ada. This Ada "source" object will eventually be translated into the machine language of the target computer. This translated Ada program also inhabits a data base object.

The APSE user can modify these data base objects in a variety of ways. One way of modifying these objects is by simply changing their names. Another way that these objects can be modified is by changing the contents of these objects. If the object contains normal English text, for instance, then this modification is usually referred to as editing.

The APSE user can use some of his tools to analyze a data base object. One result of this analysis may be the creation of another data base object. For example, one might be interested in the frequency of Ada reserved words in a particular data base object that contains some Ada program. A special tool could take this data base object as input, and produce as output another data base object that would contain a statistical table of reserved word frequency.

The APSE user can use some of his tools to change the representation of a data base object. Essentially, this means that he can create another entity from the first, with a different structure (syntax) but with the same semantics. This can be done with an Ada compiler; an Ada compiler would receive a data base object containing an Ada compilation unit as input, and produce a data base object as output that would contain the machine language representation of

41

the Ada compilation unit. Since our compiler is validated, we know that the semantics of our original Ada representation are (in a sense) unchanged.

The APSE user can use some of his tools to display a data base object in a humanly understandable fashion. There should be tools for printing the contents of a data base object on a teletypewriter or on a laser printer, or displaying it on a video display terminal.

The APSE user can consolidate separate data base objects (for example, separately compiled Ada units) into a unified object.

The APSE user can load data base objects representing Ada program units into his machine and execute them, and can also use his tools to monitor this execution.

Finally, the APSE user has available different configuration control records, showing the origin, purpose, and destiny of data base objects. Why would this be important? For an application of any complexity, control and management are necessary for high product reliability; we have seen above how this has been recognized by the professional bread bakers.

These APSE component features are part of the Stoneman requirements. Of course, they may be seen in varying degrees in other toolsets. However, we note that the underlying mechanism here is Ada and Ada only: the "spirit" of Ada encourages sharing. Consequently, APSE features must encourage the APSE user to think and work in Ada terms, not in terms of a particular host, target, operating system or other toolset which may be antithetical to the Ada goals of sharing.

Here are the names of some tools that we will examine in later chapters. Stoneman calls these tools "MAPSE tools." The MAPSE toolset consists of:

text editor
pretty printer (formatter)
translator (compiler)
linker
loader (exporter)
cross-reference
control flow
dynamic analysis ("symbolic debugging")
terminal handler
file administrator

command interpreter
configuration manager

The APSE data base also has several important characteristics. We now provide the important definitions that are concerned with the data base.

The data base is a collection of entities called objects. An object is a collection of information (its "value" or "content") and has a unique name by which it is identified. Also associated with an object is a set of attributes which provide information on the contents of the object ("meta-information") and relations which provide information on how different objects are "associated."

Objects may exist or may be created that meet the same (or closely related) specifications. These objects are called versions. Versions can be alternatives to a particular application choice (a "variation"), or updates ("revisions") to an older object.

An application may have a particular set of objects associated with it. A configuration is a data base object that represents this collection. Other groupings of data base objects are called partitions.

An APSE includes features for history preservation and configuration control. We are interested in how an object was created and which objects were used to create it. These can be recorded in history attributes and derivation attributes. This control can help to increase reliability. An an example, one source of unreliability can occur when we unintentionally change or destroy a data base object. This modification may end up affecting our entire project. One way this can be prevented is if the modification tools check the history and derivation attributes. We can even make these tools function so that we cannot easily change or destroy a data base object if it is referenced in the history attribute of another data base object.

Access control refers to the protection an object may have (e.g., passwords), so that APSE access to an object may be application specific.

One requirement of an APSE is that it should contain enough information to produce progress reports and statistical reports (with the aid of special tools). These reports can contain budgets, schedules, reviews, error fixes, implementation dates, system loading characteristics, user frequencies, and resource allocations.

Finally, the data base must be able to support various (applications oriented) backup and archive facilities.

We conclude this section by paraphrasing the STONEMAN guidelines for an APSE. An APSE is characterized by its:

SCOPE:	Development and maintenance of embedded computer systems involving Ada.
	Improvement of long-term cost-effective software reliability.
	The scope does not include general development and maintenance of computer programs in a non-Ada programming language, or for applications pertaining to large numerical algorithms, acounting, or other "nonembedded" applications.
QUALITY:	Measured reliability, performance, evolution, maintenance, responsiveness. The toolsets and application development should be managed and controlled, and have provisions for their own quality assurance.
SIMPLICITY:	Utilization of Ada concepts to promote sharing by humans.
LIFE-CYCLE:	Support applications through requirements, design, implementation, and old age.
PROJECT-TEAM:	Support project management, documentation, configuration, and release control.
USER-HELPFUL:	Easy to learn and use (syntax, semantics). Interactive tools should have an adequate response time (pragmatics).
UNIFORMITY OF PROTOCOL:	The same interfaces should be used by both humans and tools.
SYSTEM PORTABILITY:	The Stoneman sharing strategy: write APSE resources in Ada and

	isolate machine dependencies to the KAPSE.
PROJECT PORTABILITY:	An APSE should exist on more than one host so that applications can be shared.
HARDWARE:	Utilization of the technology of modern hosts: an APSE should not be limited to the "older generation" of computer hardware.
ROBUSTNESS:	Provide meaningful diagnostics and provide recovery from errors.
INTEGRATION:	Support of a common data base with uniform interfaces.
GRANULARITY:	Avoidance of resource redundancy and support of separable functions for tools.
OPEN-ENDEDNESS:	Support for resource extensibility: Old tools should be able to be improved and replaced; sets of tools should be able to be extended to newer toolsets.

References

MAPSE tools are established in Stoneman [17]. A classification of APSE tools and resources are in [32]. The property of open-endedness is discussed in [48].

Problems

1. Some Ada programmers think that the only tool they need is an Ada compiler. What support for Ada applications is not found in an Ada compiler? What support for Ada applications is not found in a "general toolset" (like your favorite operating system)?

2. Show that an APSE data base object may be written in terms of an Ada typed object.

3. Show how the functionality of APSE tools that manipulate APSE data base objects can be written in terms of Ada procedures having in, out, or in out parameters. With this analogy, show how an APSE can be considered to be an implementation of an Ada package.

5

Addendum: Formal Semantics

An APSE is very complicated to build (possibly one of the more complex software systems specified), and is also hard to understand. APSE tools and data bases have characteristics that are defined in terms of what they do and how they affect other entities. To help achieve Ada goals of sharing resources and applications, we recognize that certain APSE features may have to be specified very precisely. To achieve our Ada sharing goals, we may have to specify the exact functionality of tools, and even common practices associated with the use of these tools. Some features may have to be standardized like the Ada language. They key issue that remains is that we cannot standardize anything unless we know what it is and what it does. We now need a formal model of our Ada resources to provide unambiguous descriptions of the semantics of these resources. Once this is done, we can develop compliance documents and validation suites so that we can insure that "conforming implementations" will help us achieve the Ada sharing goals. We will examine the finer details of just what needs to be standardized in a later chapter.

One way of specifying the meaning of APSE constructs is by mapping the APSE constructs onto a formal notation and then specifying the meanings of the notation. This solution is known as providing formal semantics. The two most popular methodologies associated with formal semantics are the operational approach and the denotational approach.

The operational approach defines the meaning of a construct in terms of how these constructs affect the behavior of a particular machine. We have seen one example of this (applied to specifying the Ada language constructs) in the Ada/ED prototype Ada compiler. One problem associated with this approach is that we need to build an operational machine to help us define our constructs. Another problem is that meanings associated with constructs end up being "machine dependent." This may be tricky to apply to APSE components where we are emphasizing machine independence and portability.

The denotational approach specifies the meaning of a construct in terms of the meaning of its subconstructs (ultimately down to specifying meanings in terms of mathematical objects). An example of this is the Ada Formal Definition. Here, the Ada language constructs were mapped into an "Ada-like" notation. The meanings associated with the Ada language constructs were defined in terms of this notation; ultimately, meanings were specified in terms of mathematical sets and functions.

Denotational semantics provides a specification that is independent of a particular implementation. However, one problem is that we eventually want to specify an implementation! Because of the emphasis on implementation independence, we will utilize some of the concepts associated with denotational semantics when some tricky situations arise.

We now give two more flavors of formal semantics. Declarative semantics specifies what is being computed, not how it is being computed. Recursion is very common in a declarative specification. For example, we can give a declarative declaration of the factorial function as follows:

The factorial of zero is 1.
The factorial of n is n times the factorial of $n - 1$.

Procedural semantics specifies how an action is to be performed, step by step. A procedual specification of the factorial function is:

Initialize a counter object to *n*.

Initialize an answer object to *n*.

Decrement the counter object by 1.

Multiply the answer object by the counter object; put this new answer in the answer object.

Continue decrementing the counter, multiplying by the answer object and putting the new answer in the answer object. When the value of the counter object is 1, stop everything.

The value of *n* factorial is now contained in the answer object.

The denotational approach is usually declarative and the operational approach is usually procedural. Most "traditional" programming languages are procedural. Ada has facilities for declarative as well as procedural specifications. Most of the Ada declarative semantics are found in declarative parts (specifications) of packages, subprograms, and blocks. Procedural specification normally occurs in Ada bodies.

In an APSE, we frequently have to emphasize the distinction between a program as a declarative object (in the data base) and a program as a procedural object (when it executes). We define a process to be a representation of the procedural semantics of an Ada program: a process embodies the semantics of the machine execution of an Ada program.

In an APSE, process organization and management are similar to data base organization and management. Just as data base objects have relations and attributes, processes also have relations and attributes. The common model that has been adopted when discussing processes and data base objects is called the node model. We might say that the declarative semantics of a node represents the data base semantics and the procedural semantics of a node represents the process semantics. We will examine other details of this node model in later chapters.

We now make some concluding observations regarding denotational semantics. We have seen that denotational semantics ultimately defines the meaning of an entity in terms of what the entity does to certain sets (called domains). There are really only three basic domains:

The Store, which represents the set of allowable values that a construct may contain.

The Environment, which represents the set of allowable bindings that a construct may be named by.

The Continuation, which represents "what comes next" after the completion of a domain action.

Meanings are specified (recursively) in terms of semantic maps. These maps are certain functions that map an abstract syntax component into a special domain of answers. A complete formal specification specifies this semantic map for every possible abstract syntax configuration. This is one reason why a formal denotational semantics is tedious to develop. We can make some brief observations on the formal semantics of Ada as far as the basic domain changes are concerned (as specified above). In the Ada programming language, the Store changes after executing a command (e.g., an assignment statement). When definitions are elaborated, the Environment domain changes. Evaluation of expressions changes neither the store nor environment (in general), but it may have an affect on the Continuation domain (as in an if statement or as in raising an exception, when the "normal" flow of control changes). Other language constructs can be explained in terms of these domain constructions and semantic mappings. For example, Ada allows labels and goto statements. This means that the set of allowable values that are in the Store may depend on the Continuations. Since (in general) these Continuations depend on expression evaluation, statement execution, and definition elaboration, we observe that the Continuation domain depends on the Store and Environment. These recursive and mutually recursive definitions are part of the denotational approach.

We can try to give a denotational semantics interpretation of an APSE. The APSE has a data base which is concerned with data base objects and what they denote. This roughly corresponds to our Store and Environment. The APSE has certain interfaces which are responsible for program invocation and control. This corresponds to our Continuation domain. What corresponds to our semantic map? One correspondence can be the mapping of APSE meanings between different APSE hosts. The "equivalent semantics" associated with rehosting corresponds to the semantic map between an APSE structure(syntax) and its ultimate meanings.

Is there a need to develop a complete formal specification of an APSE? One advantage of this effort would be that all APSE users and APSE builders would know exactly what they are dealing with: a fixed, standard, unique APSE. The disadvantage (besides the extraordinary amount of labor) is seen in the Stoneman A P S E guidelines for open-endedness and hardware suport: this complete specification could limit the construction of new tools. The way out of this dilemma will be studied in greater detail in Section Five. We will show that the best answer is to specify a particular feature of an A P S E: the M A P S E-K A P S E interfaces.

References
Good references on the formal semantics of programming languages are in [49] and [51]. The denotational semantics of Ada is found in [2] and further refined in [36]. An operational semantics for Ada is in [3].

Problems
1. The Ada language can not be "subsetted" or "supersetted" without effecting its formal semantics. What about an A P S E?

2. What would be the effect on the Ada sharing goals and on the Stoneman guidelines of formally specifying an (a) A P S E, (b) M A P S E, (c) K A P S E?

3. Why is the goal of formally specifying an A P S E incompatible with the Stoneman guideline of open-endedness?

SECTION TWO
ASPECTS OF CONTROL

6

An APSE Dialog

We have already seen what the general objectives of an APSE are, and how some of these objectives can be specified by a particular philosophy of transportability and interoperability. Instead of continuing our examination of an APSE from a "top-down" viewpoint, we will now investigate a typical APSE from a "bottom-up" perspective. This will bring many of the previous abstract notions into a sharper focus. Without asking too many "why" questions, we will show exactly what a human does when he "talks" to an APSE. We emphasize that we are looking at a "typical" APSE user. He is sitting down at some kind of "typical" hardware device. During his dialog he will be making some "typical" requests to an APSE and will be controlling his requests and the APSE's actions interactively.

Because words in the pages of a book are not usually associated with the interactive devices attached to programming environments, we must make some typographical conventions.

We assume that our human APSE user is interacting solely with his APSE resources on a host computer. There is no embedded target in our initial interaction, but note that we do consider this host a target if our user is building Ada programs that execute on the host. (We will consider the more general case of distributed program development in Section 4.) We assume that we have a naive APSE user; he is probably a novice in utilizing these APSE resources to support Ada applications, but he does know the Ada language. We also assume that there is nothing really fancy about his needs or present application.

Our user is communicating through a physical device called a Video Display Terminal (VDT). We assume there is nothing fancy about this device. Our terminal has functionality similar to a typewriter (or teletypewriter) even though it may be implemented with modern television-type hardware. The terminal in turn communicates to the APSE through another device called a modem, which essentially governs the speed of communication between the human and the host computer. Our user is using a dumb terminal and a low-speed connection. In present technological language, he is using a dumb VDT that is connected to a 300 baud line.

We assume that our user has already made the appropriate physical connections between his terminal and modem and that a communication link between the modem and the APSE host has been established by dialing an appropriate telephone number or by flipping an appropriate switch. We do not care where the host is located: it can be next door or across the continent. The preliminary communications link makes the actual location of the host irrelevant.

The APSE dialog is essentially transaction based: the human types something on the terminal keyboard (which in turn is echoed on the display) and the APSE performs an action (and shows the possible effects of this action on the terminal display). Some APSE actions can be even more interactive: they could involve further requests to the human based on the context of what was previously done. The entire session is actually similar to the interaction between a human and a bank teller (who may or may not be human).

For clarity in knowing whom is talking to whom, we will represent the human commands and responses to the APSE in lowercase. The APSE response to the human will be in uppercase. What is printed here will correspond exactly to what the human sees at his terminal device. We will not print any "nonprinting" characters like "carriage-return," "line-feed," or "space." We will also annotate our dialog with "comments." These comments are meant solely for the reader of this dialog and correspond to the use of comments in Ada ("for the enlightenment of the human reader"). We assume that our APSE is smart enough to recognize comments. Our comments will look like Ada comments: anything to the right of two adjoining hyphens represents a comment. We now commence our dialog.

@login kellman ******

USER KELLMAN ACCOUNT SHUTTLE

LOGGED IN 14:27:33 1 APRIL 1985

-- The naive user talks to the host before calling the APSE.

-- The user types in his name and a "password" (given to him by
-- some administrator). The host types out (echoes) everything ex-
-- cept for this "secret" password: it types an asterisk ("*") for
-- each secret letter to prevent unauthorized access by someone
-- who may be "leaning over" our naive user's shoulder.

@

-- This symbol is the host "prompt". It tells the naive user that the
-- host is ready to process any requests.

@ada

-- A request to the host to connect the naive user to the APSE.
-- After he is identified, the APSE requests further identification:

>APSE LOGIN NAME: kellman
>APSE LOGIN PASSWORD:

'JOB(17)'SHUTTLE'USER (KELLMAN) IDENTIFIED
HELLO USER KELLMAN
THE CURRENT_NODE IS 'USER(KELLMAN)
THE CURRENT_RELATION IS 'OWNS

>

-- Again, the password is not echoed (and it may be different).
-- Our naive human user is now "logged in" to the APSE.
-- This "login" procedure establishes certain default APSE actions.
-- It also determines whether particular APSE resources
-- may be accessed by our naive user. One APSE
-- resource access control mechanism may be accomplished by
-- creating resource hierarchies. These hierarchies
-- (usually organized as a tree) manage resources by specifying
-- the nodes and paths of the tree. "Sub-trees" can be considered
-- to correspond to "users," "jobs," and controlling tools.
-- For example, in the "login" procedure, a root process
-- (a "sub-tree") is created on some APSE process tree
-- called CURRENT_JOB. This process (corresponding to the
-- anticipated procedural semantics to our user's actions)
-- can in turn spawn other processes (when programs call
-- other programs).

>time

14:27:59

>date

1-APRIL-1985

-- Some typical requests.

>dir

??? NO PROGRAM CALLED DIR.

PLEASE TYPE HELP MCL FOR HELP WITH THE COMMAND

LANGUAGE.

-- The naive user wants to list something, but is not exactly
-- sure how to do it.
-- The APSE help facility comes to the rescue.
-- However, Kellman remembers the MAPSE Command Language
-- (MCL) and tries again:

>get

GET INSUFFICIENT AND AMBIGUOUS.

TYPE GET ? FOR A LIST OF OPTIONS BEGINNING WITH GET.

>get ?

OPTIONS ARE = >

                RELATION_NAME

                ATTRIBUTE_NAME

                VARIABLE_NAME

                PARTITION

TYPE HELP GET FOR FURTHER INFORMATION.

-- Kellman remembers: he wants a partition:

>get *

    MAIL

    FOURIER

    GAUSS

    LAPLACE

    MARIE

    SUSAN

    LOG

    MESSAGE

>
-- The 'CURRENT_NODE, which we were also told is
-- 'USER(KELLMAN) is a structure node
-- (a "directory" of files).
-- This node used with certain node relations
-- can be used to access other data base objects.
-- The GET tool can be used to display the
-- names that are bound to an object. Kellman
-- remembers that the * can match all names: it can be
-- used to form a partition of objects. He uses the GET
-- tool to tell him the names of the entities in the
-- structure 'USER(KELLMAN). (He makes use of the conventions
-- and defaults regarding the 'CURRENT_NODE and
-- 'CURRENT_RELATION.)

-- Kellman is interested in finding out more about the
-- data base objects in this directory. He
-- now wants to know what attributes are available to him
-- in order to access the "meta-knowledge" of the
-- FOURIER data base object. This can be accomplished
-- by requesting the names of the attributes of FOURIER:

>get fourier'* --   What are FOURIER's attributes?

PURPOSE

CREATED_BY

DERIVED_ FROM

ACCESS

NODE_TYPE ˆo   --   The user types "control-o"
                --   to stop the listing.

--   What is the purpose of FOURIER?
>list fourier' purpose

FOURIER'PURPOSE =>

FAST FOURIER TRANSFORM FOR 2-D

IMAGE RECOGNITION

>
--   The naive user asks what is the purpose of data base object called
--   fourier. This is accomplished by listing the contents of
--   its purpose attribute.

>lst$ = LIST ˆu   --   A legal abbreviation, followed by an "$"
                   --   (escape) for automatic "fill in,"
                   --   and then a "control-u" to ignore the line.
                   --   Type a "carriage return" and start again.

>

>list (object => marie, attribute => purpose)

MARIE'PURPOSE =>

61

INVITATION TO MOVIE

-- Commands may also be given with "Ada-like syntax."
-- The contents of the attribute are listed.

>l marie

??? L INSUFFICIENT AND AMBIGUOUS.

TYPE L? FOR A LIST OF OPTIONS BEGINNING WITH L

PLEASE TYPE HELP MCL FOR HELP WITH THE COMMAND LANGUAGE

-- An abbreviation that is evidently forbidden by this
-- command language.

>lst marie   --   An acceptable abbreviation: extension with $ not
              --   necessary. The contents of MARIE are listed.

Dear Marie,

    I was wondering if you were free Thursday night,

to see Gone with the Wind?

Kellman

>create (example_dir, node_type = > structure)

-- The naive user makes another data base object that can contain
-- other data base objects. These objects are sometimes called
-- directories or structures and correspond to certain "local root"
-- nodes in our data base hierarchy.

>get *

MAIL

FOURIER

GAUSS

LAPLACE

MARIE

SUSAN

LOG

MESSAGE

EXAMPLE_DIR

>list (object = >example_dir, attribute = >node_type)

EXAMPLE_DIR'NODE_TYPE = >

STRUCTURE

>set_current_node example_dir
  -- Move to the created directory.

>Edit

SLOW EDITOR VERSION 314159

-- An invocation of the editor. Note the different editor prompt:

-- Kellman inserts a package specification.

E>i

package A is

function Inc(X:Integer) return Integer;

end A;

-- Termination of inserted text.

E>;w$ =WRITE_TO_OBJECT=>spec
   -- More automatic fill-in.

      PURPOSE=> simple example of package specification

##

-- Termination of this editor command:
-- Kellman has finished editing.
-- He writes the text in the object called spec.

E>;k$ =KILL_BUFFER ##

-- He erases whatever the editor stored locally in its "buffer"
-- and starts again:

E>i

package body A is

function inc(x:integer)return

integer is begin return x+1; end; end; ##

E>;w$ =WRITE_OBJECT=>body

      PURPOSE= > body of package A ##

-- The tool that will reformat this object so that
-- it is easier on the eyes is called a formatter.

E>e$ = exit##

-- A request to leave the editor.

> -- Back to the APSE command language.

-- Kellman wants to reformat the Ada text inside body
-- with a simple invocation of the Ada format tool:

>format (old_ada = >body, formatted_ada = >body_pp)

>list body_pp -- list the contents of this "pretty-printed" file:

package body A is

function INC (X: INTEGER) return INTEGER is

begin

return X + 1;

end;

end;

-- Kellman now wants to create a main program that will use

65

--   other compilation units. He needs the editor again.
--   (But this time he types a little more neatly.)

>edit

SLOW EDITOR VERSION 314159

E>i

with A; with Text_IO;

procedure Output is

        X:Integer;

        package MY_IO is new Integer_IO(Num = >Integer);

        use MY_IO;

begin

        for N in 1 . . 2 loop

          New_Line;

          Put("Input X "); Get (X); Set_Col(20);

          Put(A.Inc(X));

          end loop;

end Output;

##

E>;w$ = WRITE_TO_OBJECT = >main

        PURPOSE = >main program example using library package
        ##
E>;k$ = KILL_BUFFER##

-- Kellman wants to create another text.
-- Now he prepares an APSE "script";

```
E>i                          -- Ask for an input file name:

list "input file?"           -- list content of the string;

set input_file_name, read    -- define a variable and set it
                             -- to the next input stream value.

run_prog in = > input_file_name

##

E>;w$ = WRITE_OBJECT = >script

        PURPOSE = > to show actions of the command language
        processor

##
```

-- This script asks for an input file name. This file is
-- then used as the Ada STANDARD_INPUT file for the program
-- called run_prog.

```
E>;e$ = exit##
```

-- Kellman leaves the editor.

```
>get * -- The names of objects bound to 'CURRENT_NODE
       -- are listed:
```

SPEC

BODY

MAIN

SCRIPT

BODY_PP

-- The naive user wants to run these Ada programs but is not sure
-- how to do it.

>compile ?

FIRST PARAMETER: ADA_SOURCE_FILE

SECOND_PARAMETER: ADA_LIBRARY_NODE

TYPE ? FOR OTHER PARAMETERS

TYPE HELP COMPILE FOR FURTHER INFORMATION

>COMPILE ^u -- Oops! He says forget it because he does not have
             -- a program library: he must first make one with
             -- the library tool.

>library -- Invocation of the library tool: note the new prompt:

L>create (name = >ex_lib, target = >host)

--   A library structure is created called ex_lib.
--   This will contain all compilation, run-time support routines,
--   and ultimately, machine instructions for the target specified,
--   which in this case is the host.

L>set ex_lib'read , 'user(kellman)

--   The naive user is preventing others from using this library.

L>exit   --   Leave the library tool.

--   Now we can compile:

>compile spec,ex_lib

--   wait for the program (tool) called compile to finish

>   --   finished

>compile(source = >body,

        library = >ex_lib,

        when = > background)

'JOB(23) EXECUTING

--   When compiling in background mode, we do not have to wait
--   (as distinct from the previous foreground mode).
--   We can do other things, like find out about the last foreground
--   job where the user compiled spec:

>list apse.execution_time'last_foreground

--   Kellman uses a predefined APSE name.

69

2.546 MINUTE

-- Is job(23) finished?

,>list 'job(23)'terminated   -- A predefined attribute of pro-
                                    -- cesses.

        NO

  -- The answer is no. The naive user checks again:

>list 'job(23)'terminated

          NO

-- This is getting tedious. Time for some games:

>list "hello"

         HELLO

>

-- Finally, we are told:

>   'JOB(23) TERMINATED

>list 'job (23)' terminated

         YES

>list 'job(23)'execution_time

         3.987 MINUTE

>compile main,

        ex_lib,

background   --   since "carriage returns" usually
                    --   terminate commands in this com-
                    --   mand language, we can use a
                    --   "comma" to denote the continua-
                    --   tion of a command to the next line.
                    --   This is useful if an invoked program
                    --   needs several parameters.

'JOB(9) EXECUTING

>get *

SPEC

BODY

MAIN

SCRIPT

BODY_PP

EX_LIB

--   Now Kellman wants to read his mail: note the prompt—

>mail_man

READING 'USER(KELLMAN).MAIL

NO NEW MESSAGES

--   Kellman's mailbox is denoted with the default
--   relation (indicated by ".") from his top structure node.

M>s$ = SEND_MESSAGE

71

-- A command of a command in another "command language."
-- Note the double prompt:

M>S>   TO: deluca@un-fao

           CC: kellman

           SUBJECT: important note:please respond

           MESSAGE:?

       OPTIONS ARE: COMPOSE

                   EXIT

                   EDIT

       FOR OTHER OPTIONS TYPE ?

       FOR HELP ON THE SEND COMMAND TYPE HELP SEND.

       M>S>   MESSAGE: compose

               -- Kellman wants to write a new letter.
               -- He can either write the message in right here or read it in
               -- as a file:

           M>S>C>   FILE OR TEXT

           M>S>C>file

               PATH_NAME:'user(kellman).marie

> TYPE ## WHEN DONE
> -- If you want to add anything else:

p.s. It starts around 7:30. ##

-- Kellman specifies the marie object with the default relation name.

M>S>send

-- Kellman tells the mail tool to send the letter.
-- This also gets him out of the send "subcommand."

> DELUCA@UN-FAO SENT

> KELLMAN SENT

*** YOU HAVE NEW MAIL FROM KELLMAN ***

-- Kellman knows what the message is; he leaves the mail tool.

M>exit

>list apse.last_background

-- Kellman forgot who was running.

> 'JOB(9)

>list'job(9)'terminated

> YES

-- Kellman knows he must link and export:

>link(main_program = >output,

> library = >ex_lib,

> output_object = >linked_ex)

73

```
--   The link tool helps identify the main program. The linked object
--   is placed in the library as the library data base object
--   called linked_ex.
```

```
>export(linked_object = >linked_ex,

          library = >ex_lib,

          target_output = >my_exe)
```

```
--   Kellman wants to see what changes he has now made to his direc-
--   tory: He first checks to see what objects are under configuration
--   control:
```

```
>get *'(configuration_control => yes)

          SPEC

          BODY

          SCRIPT

          MAIN

          EX_LIB
```

```
--   These objects have versions that are stored in the data base. This
--   APSE has the convention that a reference to these configuration
--   controlled objects is a reference to the last version of the object.
```

```
>get *'version(*)   --   What are the numbers of the versions of
                    --   my files?


          SPEC'VERSION(1)
```

BODY'VERSION(1)

SCRIPT'VERSION(1)

MAIN'VERSION(1)

EX_LIB'VERSION(1)

```
--   Since he did not modify any existing file in the current node,
--   all files have version 1. Other versions could have been
--   created if an existing file was modified.
--   We can check the versions of library files in a similar manner:
```

```
>library ex_lib   --   Invoke library tool with library ex_lib.
```

```
L>get *
```

A

OUTPUT

LINKED_EX

```
--   Library structures that denote Ada compilation units.
--   The actual library files are leaves of these structures
--   and can be obtained with the iterate tool:
```

```
L>iterate *
```

A'SPEC'VERSION(1)

A'BODY'VERSION(1)

OUTPUT'BODY' VERSION(1)

LINKED_EX'VERSION(1)

-- A list of all the versions of the compiled compilation units
-- and linked objects. This list could also have been obtained with
-- the get tool by: get *'*'version(*).

L>exit

>list script

        LIST "INPUT_FILE ?"

        SET INPUT_FILE_NAME, READ

        RUN_PROG IN = > INPUT_FILE_NAME

-- Kellman has found an error.

>edit script

E>srun#-3dddddd#imy_exe##

E>0tt##

E>   MY_EXE IN = > INPUT_FILE_NAME

E>;s$ = SAVE

        SCRIPT'VERSION(2)

        REASON_FOR_REVISION = > wrong file
          name--runprog

##

E>exit##

>get script'version(*)

SCRIPT'VERSION(1)

SCRIPT'VERSION(2)

-- When Kellman refers to the file script, which version is it?
-- He can easily find out:

>list script

LIST "INPUT_FILE?"

SET INPUT_FILE_NAME, READ

MY_EXE IN => INPUT_FILE_NAME

-- This command language references the LAST version.

-- Now the user can finally run his Ada program:
>script

INPUT FILE ? standard_input

INPUT X 2   3

INPUT X 5   6

-- Finished!

-- Now Kellman also has a friend who is also a naive APSE user:
-- this friend has two files, friend_nos and friend_files. Kellman
-- has read access to these files:

>list 'user(deluca). friend_files

       'USER(DELUCA).FRIEND_NOS

>list 'user(deluca).friend_nos

       97 98

--   Kellman wants to play with input-output redirection:

>create (results, node_type = >file)

  --   Creating a file without the editor.

>script in = >'user(deluca).friend_files out = > results,

                     when = > background

       'JOB(54) EXECUTING

--   Wait for it to finish:

>

       'JOB(54) TERMINATED

>list results

       INPUT FILE ?

       INPUT X   98

       INPUT X   99

--   At this point, Kellman has had enough. He terminates his "root
--   process" with the "logout" tool. This tool does the necessary
--   "housekeeping" to enable Kellman to leave.

>logout

GOODBYE USER KELLMAN

DIAGNOSTICS HAVE BEEN APPENDED TO THE FILE

'USER(KELLMAN).MESSAGE

THIS SESSION HAS BEEN APPENDED TO THE FILE

'USER(KELLMAN).LOG

```
--   Messages sent by tools have been recorded to the message file;
--   a "transcript" that recorded everything that Kellman just did
--   was appended to Kellman's log file.


@   --   Kellman now mistakenly leaves his terminal.
    --   (He is still logged into the host!)
```

References

The issues behind various A P S E command languages are discussed in [4], [5], [6], [7], [8], [9], [10]. The node model for processes and data objects is found in [15].

Problems

1. Translate this "typical" A P S E dialog into a "typical" dialog with your favorite operating system or (non-Ada) programming support environment.

2. List all tools that were invoked by the human in this dialog. Which tools would be classified as M A P S E tools? Which wouldn't be?

3. How would this dialog change if (a) no host login was necessary, or (b) it was first necessary to login to a computer network.

4. Identify the Ada files STANDARD_INPUT, STANDARD_OUTPUT, and MESSAGE_OUTPUT for all tools that were invoked.

5. What are three good reasons for having an A P S E create a log file?

7

APSE
Control Interface
Requirements

One of Stoneman's objectives is that the control interface should be independent of the host computer: it should be a "virtual" interface. What do we mean by virtual? In our layered military paradigm, a virtual interface corresponds to an officer giving the same orders to (a) the troops that he trained with, (b) troops that were trained by some other officer, or (c) troops (in the same army) residing halfway around the world. The important concept here is that when the officer issues orders, his inferiors will obey regardless of whoever or wherever they are. In more general terms, the virtual interface corresponds to a "standard" communication link between levels; the commands given from the superior level to the inferior level are in some sense "independent" of the actual identity of the inferior level. This virtual interface therefore leads to the transportability of the higher levels of command.

The APSE also utilizes the concept of virtual interface when we consider the Stoneman layered model. We now examine this interface as an APSE resource that can be shared.

If we want the control interface to be a shared resource, then we conclude that the interface must be part of the MAPSE. This would also help solve our transportability and interoperability requirements since this interface would be written in Ada and have host dependencies isolated to the KAPSE interfaces. Stoneman specifies that the "human end" of the control interface should be expressed in a simple and understandable language. (As far as Stoneman is concerned, this language may even resemble the syntax and semantics of Ada.) This would also help achieve the human guidelines of portability.

Part of the control interface is concerned with the human control interaction over a tool. Another part of the interface also governs how tools react with other tools. Stoneman specifies that one kind of very important tool interaction occurs when tools are "composed" (like mathematical functions) to create other tools. A primitive invoking facility must be available that "calls" tools from within other tools. Finally Stoneman also requires a way to build "job control sequences" which can in turn initiate other programs, other tools, and other job control sequences.

The MAPSE tool that realizes many of these objectives is called a command language processor (CLP). The "job control language" that this tool supplies is called the command language (also called the MAPSE Command Language, or MCL). We emphasize that a command language is a notation for specifying interactive control over APSE tool interfaces. We also emphasize that the CLP is a MAPSE tool, and therefore is written in Ada.

Since the MCL is a notation we can specify algorithms in it. The specification of particular algorithms that control APSE tool interfaces (the "job control sequence") is called a script. Scripts are written in the command language. Scripts may also be stored in a data base object. (They are therefore functionally equivalent to Ada programs.) And, according to Stoneman, there must be a mechanism for invoking and controlling scripts! Scripts can control tools, programs, and other scripts.

One natural question to ask is: Can scripts built on one APSE be shared on another APSE? One answer is given by the Stoneman sharing strategy:

1. Recompile the CLP on the other APSE (host) after identifying the CLP-KAPSE interfaces.

2. Run the script unchanged on the rehosted CLP.

There are two traditional ways that scripts may be invoked and controlled by a human. One way is to have the invoker personally invoke the script. In this case, the invoker must wait for the script to complete execution before doing anything else. This is frequently seen in a roomfull of time-shared computer terminals. In such a room, the humans are waiting for the computer to schedule their job to allocate computer resources. Waiting time is thus split up between the time that the computer actually takes to process the job and the time it takes to schedule and allocate its resources.

Another way of invoking and controlling scripts is to have the invoker invoke his job and then be able to do something else. He may simply leave the terminal room, confident that his "submitted" or "batch" job will be processed, or he may invoke other jobs (included here is checking if a script is finished or not).

The first case is called foreground mode invocation and the second case is called background mode invocation. We note that background mode invocation can, in turn, invoke many concurrent tool, program, and script executions.

We can use Ada tasks to help us model situations of concurrent processes. In one situation, Ada tasks usually communicate by rendezvous: the task that issues an entry call is suspended until the entry is accepted by the serving task. The "calling" task is suspended and its life resumes only after the rendezvous. Another situation is seen when a task object is created as a result of an access object allocation. This allocation can occur at run time, and can also be associated with the actions of another task. In this situation, the created tasks execute concurrently with all other tasks.

In the APSE there are two similar situations. These situations also formalize our notions of invocation and control. The first situation is when a calling process is suspended until the called process completes. We define this situation as one of process invocation. The second situation is when a calling process is not suspended until the called process completes. We define this situation as one of process spawning. Both of these situations should be seen in the MCL.

We now consider five basic requirements for the command language:

1. The CLP is a tool; consequently, it can be invoked by the command language. Since the LRM tells us that "A main program acts as if called by some [Ada Programming

Support] environment task," we can consider the CLP as just another Ada task. In the APSE process model, the CLP (considered as a process) can invoke or spawn other processes, including itself.

2. The MCL should support the Ada concepts for input, output, and control.

3. The calling conventions of programs, tools, and scripts should be syntactically the same.

4. Who can call who? If "A→B" is an abbreviation for "The Process denoted by A calls the Process denoted by B," then the following calling scenarios are possible:

> program→tool
> program→script
> program→program
>
> tool→program
> tool→script
> tool→tool
>
> script→program
> script→tool
> script→script

5. Commands should not be cryptic and unreadable.

The last point embroils us in a popular controversy: readability versus writability. On the "pro" side for short and cryptic language are the clever, experienced users (sometimes called hackers): Why should they have to type slowly when they can type commands at a quick rate? This school of thought believes that the best program (or script) is the shortest program (or script). This implies that one should do his utmost to take advantage of abbreviations.

Everyone else seems to be against the short, cryptic commands in favor of more "readable" syntax. They say this style is bad for the inexperienced. They also say that scripts frequently have long lifetimes so they should be understandable, especially by people who did not write them.

One possible compromise includes the following. We can allow certain legal abbreviations of longer names. A special command should be available to "fill in" these abbreviations if that is desired. Large scripts should not be encouraged: if a large script must be written that is that important to the application, it should be written in Ada if one desires to take advantage of Ada's features of readability, reliability, and maintainability.

Another popular controversy is presented with the following question: Why can't Ada itself be the command language? Since scripts would in fact be Ada programs, wouldn't it make the transportability problem of scripts trivial? There would be a complete and uniform syntax between the calling scenarios of tools, programs, and scripts. Wouldn't this satisfy the Stoneman guideline of uniformity? Using Ada as an MCL would also result in very understandable (and not cryptic) scripts. Besides, there is some legacy in using a programming language as a command language. Stoneman mentions Interlisp in this regard, as a programming language that is also a command language.

This may work for some APSE users, but it seems that the majority of APSE users do not want Ada as an MCL. First of all, this would be using Ada in a different application domain than was intended: Ada was designed to specify algorithms in embedded computer systems, not for specifying algorithms that control APSE interfaces! (This does not mean that Ada "can't" do it, it just means that using Ada for this purpose may be awkward.) We may ask if this means that Ada is not the right language to write an APSE. Since the key goal of the entire Ada effort is to encourage the sharing of resources, and one method of accomplishing this is by standardizing a common language, we must conclude that the APSE must be written in Ada if the APSE resources are to be shared.

A second point against using Ada as an MCL is that Ada emphasizes readability and does not allow abbreviations that seem to be common among command languages.

Our third point is concerned with language semantics. A CLP is usually implemented as an interpreter. An interpreter translates its programs line by line (or command by command). Ada is implemented by a compiler. As we saw previously a compiler translates an entire program into a whole set of machine instructions. The semantics associated with compiled Ada may be different from interpreted Ada semantics. Conversely, using compiled Ada as the MCL may present terrible overhead problems (especially knowing the performance benchmarks for present Ada compilers).

Our final point presents the most important objection to using Ada an an MCL. We simply go back to the reasons why we said we needed an APSE in the first place: the Ada language simply does not provide enough support for "environmental" issues. For example, Ada does not have any mechanism that enables Ada programs to invoke other Ada programs (indeed, there are even some fuzzy language issues about the nature of Ada main programs). As we observed in Section 1, Ada simply leaves too many important details up to the implementation for it to be an adequate MCL.

One compromise is to build a command language that utilizes Ada syntax to a certain extent and extends Ada semantics in some ways while restricting it considerably in other ways. Ada concepts will be used to explain the MCL actions. We finally note that just as Ada incorporated many good concepts from other programming languages, the MCL will incorporate many good concepts from the command languages of other programming environments.

We now briefly get back to the human invoker of APSE resources. We know that the human can invoke programs, tools, and scripts by the facilities provided by the MCL. But what exactly does the human physically interact with? The essential device is called a terminal. It consists of:

A keyboard that supports the Ada lexical set. Just as in Ada, we specify that uppercase and lowercase is not significant in the MCL.

A display that ranges in quality and functionality from a teletypewriter to a high-resolution bit-mapped graphic display. These displays are sometimes referred to as either "smart" or "dumb." One reason is that the speed at which these devices are connected can determine the pragmatic functionality of many tools.

Other devices that may input or output sound, motion, and so on. These include devices like a light-pen and a mouse which are not associated with the Minimal APSE but may be associated with special APSE tools.

Why are these devices important? One reason is that they are frequently instantiations of what Ada defines as STANDARD_INPUT, STANDARD_OUTPUT, and MESSAGE_OUTPUT. In other words, input is usually recieved from the terminal keyboard, and output is usually sent to the terminal display. STANDARD_INPUT, STANDARD_OUTPUT, and MESSAGE_OUTPUT could also denote APSE data base objects. In this case, input and output can be associated with other (noninteractive) devices that correspond to a memory (such as magnetic disk or tape).

At the terminal, the human should have the power to start, stop and restart whatever he can invoke. This power should be available to him in either foward or background mode. The human should also be able to get special "meta-information" about whatever process is executing. How exactly would this be done? There may be certain MCL keywords or special characters that enable such interrogations to occur. This will be examined in the next chapter.

References

MCL requirements are in Stoneman [17]. Interesting discussions on using Ada as on MCL are found in [4]; for a dissenting view, see [54]. Some observations on interactive devices and their functionality with respect to the MCL are in [20] and [25].

Problems

1. List the advantages and disadvantages of using an "Ada-subset" as an MCL.

2. In the APSE dialog in Chapter 6, identify which programs were invoked or spawned. Identify who called who.

3. Can you specify the character set of an APSE keyboard?

8

Command Language Processors

The MAPSE command language processor (CLP) interprets programs (scripts) that are written in the MAPSE command language (MCL). In some ways, an MCL program is like a sequence of machine instructions. A program consists of a set of short, basic instructions that directly control the internal domains of a machine. No translation process that changes the representation of the MCL program (like compilation) is performed.

In other ways, the MCL is like Ada. The MCL is capable of performing some sophisticated actions. In some ways it even "looks" like Ada.

We now investigate the syntax and semantics associated with a MAPSE command language. As before, we take a bottom-up view of what is going on inside the MCL. At the lowest level, the MCL is made up of lexical units. These consist of identifiers, special characters, and some special symbols. This area is where the MCL resembles Ada the most. MCL lexical units and Ada lexical units are identical. This can eliminate some tedious time for humans who are learning the MCL for the first time. However, we still have the problems associated with semantics. The semantics of the lexical units may be different for different MAPSE command languages.

Before we discuss the detailed specifications of MCL semantics, we first observe some general matters. One matter that we should presently resolve is the readability-writability controversy as far as the abbreviation of "long" names is concerned. Experienced people like to abbreviate; abbreviation saves them time. Others (especially those who are learning) need to know exactly what is going on: for them, abbreviation (in the beginning) may be tedious and time-consuming if it tends to make them make mistakes. The most flexible (but hardest to implement) alternative is to provide a long form, provide some "intelligent" abbreviations for the long form, and to provide an expansion mechanism that would expand a cryptic abbreviation into a long form that captures the intentions of the writer. An identifier written in these three ways would denote the same meanings; only the form would be different. For example,

list example

lst example

ls$ = LIST example

the identifiers "list", "lst", and "ls$" denote the same thing, and where the "$" is a special command to the CLP that has the effect of "filling-in" the typed-in abbreviation (as indicated by the " = ").

Another issue associated with the semantics of certain lexical units is their traditional use as exception handlers. Humans make mistakes, especially typing mistakes. When the human becomes aware that he has made a mistake (an exception was raised), he tries to correct that mistake as soon as possible. Special commands are typed to correct the situation. These typed commands also are never confused with the normal continuation associated with the human text input. The traditional exception handlers are denoted by special "control" characters in package ASCII (see LRM, page C-4). Most terminal keyboards do not have enough keys to represent all 128 characters: what is usually done is that certain keys denote "switches." Hence, a keyboard with 32 keys, a shift key (switch), and a control key (switch) can represent 128 different characters. The special "control" characters are typed by holding a control key simultaneously with another key. (For example, the ASCII control character BEL can be typed by holding the control key and simultaneously pressing the G key.) Here are some examples of control characters and their semantics:

ˆu   ignore the line presently being typed

<del> ignore the character just typed

ˆr   echo the present line (type it over)

ˆc   interrupt last MCL command and ignore it

ˆb   break-in command for suspension of current process and presentation of option list

Some other lexical elements that are used for exception handlers are:

$ fill in an abbreviation or make sense out of something cryptic

?   ask for a set of available choices

<return> usually a MCL command terminator (like Ada ";")

,   signals the MCL that the present command continues on the

next line

Identifiers are lexical elements that can denote names. Names can be

variables, like input_file;
reserved words (keywords), like compile or read;
predefined attributes, like 'terminated;
pathnames to objects, like 'user(kellman).marie'version(1);
partitions,   like 'user(*).*_documentation
or 'user(˜ ˜ ˜ man).* (where the ˜ matches
any single character, and the * matches any
group of characters)

Sequences of special characters can denote
    prompts   E>
    redirection:
                input and output redirection

                        in = >

                        out = >

                execution redirection

                        = >forward

                        = >backward

    concurrent execution   -|-

  Ada equivalences

            named parameter   = >

            range . .

            equality predicates = , / = , > = , < =

            comments   --

Keywords can be used for control. Some denote actions that change the local store and environment of the APSE session. This includes

assignment:

>set input_file, data.ada

>set APSE.prompt, ada->

ada->get input_file

            YES   --   There is a name bound to this variable.

ada->list input_file

DATA.ADA   --   List the name denoted by input_file.

The MCL is not Ada. One important distinction is that variable names do not have to be defined before they are used. This is easily accomplished with an interpreter but does not correspond to the semantics of Ada, where variables must be defined before they are used.

Assignment can be used for data base object literals or for command expressions: essentially we are only dealing with string manipulation. For example, we may write:

> set com compile library = >my_lib,

                    source_file = >

> com my_main

-- If we try, we can be very cryptic.

Some commands affect continuations and are very similar to the Ada "control structures."

> if file'attention = urgent then

        compile file ex_lib

    elsif file'attention = documentation then

        list file, out = > my_doc

                -- List contents of file (to my_doc).

    else get file'*

            -- Otherwise, type out the attributes of
            -- file (to STANDARD_OUTPUT).

    end if

>

93

```
--   loop mechanisms

>    for k in 1 . . 3 loop

         list k out = > ex_nos

     --   type 1 2 3 in file ex_nos

     end loop

>


>    while a < = 4 loop

         set s s + 1

         if s > = a then

             exit

         end if

     end loop

>


--   compound commands

>    my_block:    begin

                  set f, read   --   From STANDARD_INPUT.

                  get f'*   --   What attributes are
                            --   defined for f?

                  list f'*   --   List them on
                             --   STANDARD_OUTPUT.

                  end   ,
```

    in = >' user(kellman).testin,

    out = >' user(kellman).testout

-- Redirect input-output for block;
-- entire command terminated by last "carriage-return"

-- Execution redirection:

> compile (main.ex_lib)

-- In foreground mode, we wait for it to finish.

>

> compile (main,ex_lib, background)

    'JOB(33) EXECUTING

> -- In background mode,we do not have to wait for it to finish.

--   Input-output redirection and concurrency:

> script ,

    in = > friends.files,

    out = > results

-- The data base object friends.files is now the
-- standard input to the program called script.
-- The data base object result is now the
-- standard output to the program called script.

> script -l- print

-- A special command "abbreviation" in our MCL.
-- The standard input to the program called script is the
-- default standard input.
-- (As we observed, usually the terminal.)

```
--   The output of the program called script is then input to
--   the program called print. The output of the program called
--   print is once again the default standard output.
--   This is similar to
```

>my_pipe:

        begin

                script   ,

                        out = >temporary_file

                print ,

                        in = >temporary_file

        end

    >

We do not mean to exhaust all possible features of an MCL. Of course some MAPSE command languages will have more features (and thus be considered "more powerful") than other command languages. For example, in some MCLs, scripts can have parameters passed to them. A special script of this kind would look just like an Ada subprogram. This facility would be very powerful since one can create parameterized programs and tools by parameterizing scripts.

Other MCL syntactical units govern process invocation and control. We recall that a process is the actual machine realization of an Ada program, implemented with machine instructions and run-time computing resources. These processes can start, can be suspended, and can be restarted. These processes can also be queried about their status. Here are some examples:

```
>   compile me mylib

--   A process is executing but we must wait for it to finish.
```

    ^C

-- An abort command: the process is interrupted and
-- the invocation ignored.

>

-- In the background:

> compile me mylib background

           'JOB(45) EXECUTING   --   the invoked program is
                                      --   denoted by process
                                      --   'JOB(45)
                                      --   (an "environment task")

>   --   We are ready for other actions,like

>   suspend 'job(45)   --   halt the program

>   --   other actions

>   resume 'job(45)   --   continue execution where we left it

>   abort 'job(45)   --   kill the program

           'JOB(45) ABORTED

-- Other control actions include:

>compile me mylib background

           'JOB(39) EXECUTING

>

>   wait 'job(39)   --   This causes the CLP to wait
                            --   for completion of the program,
                            --   like putting it in foreground mode.

           'JOB(39) TERMINATED

Here is an example of the use of suspend and resume in foreground mode:

```
>   loop

    set a, read in => my_input

    list a

    suspend here

    end loop
```

```
98   --   The name a was set to this object
     --   which was read from my_input
```

```
HERE SUSPENDED      --   The name here contains the
                    --   continuation associated
                    --   with where the script loop
                    --   halted. We are free to do
                    --   other actions:
```

```
>list "hello"

        HELLO

>list a

        98
```

We now wish to resume the process associated with the name here:

```
>   resume here

        99

        HERE SUSPENDED

>   --  And so on.
```

A suspended program returns control to its invoker, while saving the continuation in an APSE node. This object can be contained in the current node of the user. This could be a very helpful feature:

if an APSE user has to leave the APSE for a length of time and does not want to lose his processes, he can suspend them and store them in his data base. These processes (in "suspended animation") can then be resumed the next time the user enters the APSE.

Since the CLP is a program, it too can be invoked and suspended! If we are at the MCL prompt level and suspended the CLP, control is returned to whoever invoked the CLP. If the CLP invoked itself, we return back to the original (invoker) CLP. In the case that the CLP was invoked by the login tool (through the host), the CLP is suspended and control returns to the host; the user has now left the APSE. The more conventional way of leaving the APSE and terminating an APSE dialog is to use the logout tool.

The logout tool is an "inverse" to the login tool. We have seen that when an APSE user logs in to the APSE, he is assigned certain root nodes. In particular, a root process node is created from which all other invoked processes are controlled. These processes do not have to wait for the termination of the user's spawned processes (background execution).

When the user logs out, this root node and all other nodes in the process tree are deleted. "Bookkeeping" processes are invoked to achieve this. In some MAPSE command languages, the APSE user can create his own bookkeeping functions. This can be accomplished at login by creating "login scripts," and at logout by creating "logout scripts."

We summarize this section by mentioning how the status of running programs can be checked.

Associated with Ada is a predefined environment of identifiers and their denotations. The same is true of the MCL. Many of these names are contained in the data base object APSE, which is accessable to every MAPSE user. The MAPSE user can use this predefined environment, and may even be able to redefine the environment during his APSE session. Here are some examples:

>set APSE.prompt ADA IS WAITING:

ADA IS WAITING: list apse.last_foreground

       'JOB(56) --   Get the name of the last
              --   invoked foreground process.

ADA IS WAITING: list 'job(56)'execution_time

    3.1416 MINUTE   --   How long it took.

ADA IS WAITING: list 'job(56)'exit_status

    EXECUTION INTERRUPTED   --   What happened.

ADA IS WAITING: list APSE.last_background

    'JOB(23)   --   Get the name of the
               --   last background process.

ADA IS WAITING: list APSE.all_background

    'JOB(23)

    'JOB(26)

    'JOB(5)

ADA IS WAITING: list 'job(23)'terminated

    YES   --   Did process 23 finish? Yes.

ADA IS WAITING: list 'job(23)'exit_status

    NORMAL   -- Anything unusual? No.

Why is the CLP different from other interactive APSE tools or programs? Many interactive tools can be considered to have a "command language" of their own. These tools include debuggers, editors, and mail tools. We will discuss the properties of some of these APSE tools in later chapters.

References
The ideas behind our model of a MAPSE command language were consolidated from [4], [5], [6], [8]. Many of the interesting observations about command languages can be found in [20], [25], [38], [40], [41], [46].

Problems
1. Write two sets of MCL scripts, one "legible" and one "illegible." (You may define your own abbreviations.)

2. Does the MCL outlined here meet the Stoneman guideline of (a) granularity, (b) uniformity?

3. An APSE process does not have to execute on a single processor. Does this conflict with the Ada definition of multiprocessor Ada task execution?

9

Editors and Integrated Environments

An editor is a MAPSE tool that is actually characterized by its own (command) language. In fact, an editor may be thought of as a highly specialized CLP. We can think of the editor as a CLP that invokes and controls the editing facilities as "tools." We will examine the issues associated with the MAPSE editor and the nature of the invocation of the editing "tools." We also will consider the functionality of the editor tool vis-a-vis device functionality. These investigations equally apply to other tools: it is convenient to specify the editor as a "typical" interactive tool on which we can concentrate. Interactive tools (and editors in particular) are the tools with which programmers spend most of their time. A careful analysis of these tools can then give us some ideas for "human" portability.

There really are three types of editors. These editors correspond to the physical devices that interface with the human. We call these editors the dumb editor, the display editor, and the integrated editor. As far as the Stoneman requirements are concerned, all three editors must be capable of the following "word processing" operations. Again, we can think of these operations as commands to a CLP:

find
A given text can be located.

alter
A given text can be changed.

insert
A given text can be placed in another given text.

delete
A given text can be erased.

format
A given text can be restructured.

input
The contents of a data base object can be sent to the editor.

output
The contents of the editor can be sent to a data base object.

move
A given text can be erased and inserted in another place.

copy
A given text can be duplicated.

substitute
A given text can be replaced by another given text.

The basic abstract model of an editor is that a copy of the text (to be edited) is read into an area of storage called a buffer. All editing changes are then made to this buffer. For these changes to become permanent, the buffer must be "written" back into the original text. The buffer is characterized by its ability of locating characters and strings. All three editors can perform the same operations and can be modelled with the behavior of a buffer. However, the editors differ considerably in their ease of use and ease of learning.

Dumb editors operate on streams of characters. After a command, we do not know what the buffer looks like exactly, although a command can be given to display the buffer or portions of the buffer. These editors have distinct "insert" commands. Dumb editors are notorious for being cryptic and difficult to learn. However, it can be observed that many humans who are used to a particular dumb editor are very reluctant to give another editor a chance, even when the other editor is easier to use. (Perhaps this is because of the fear of learning another cryptic language, or because dumb editors, by being so primitive, are really very powerful. Dumb editors are also highly flexible and can be used with the simplest of devices.)

One important note regarding dumb editors: what we see on the screen is not what we get. The dumb editor usually has displayed a combination of original text, editing commands, edited text, and prompts, all of which look confusing to the uninitiated.

Display editors make full use of a VDT terminal. The VDT display is used as a "window" into the buffer. Editing changes performed on the buffer are immediately displayed and appear almost instantly (if the terminal device is connected to a reasonably fast communication line).

One problem associated with display editors is the ability in distinguishing between the text and editing commands. There is no insert command: text typed in is entered into the buffer. Certain characters, not normally used for text input (like control characters), are frequently used as prefixes for editing commands. These commands can also be displayed to the human in a special region on the VDT display that the editor sets up (sometimes called the command window). Display editors are easy to learn and convenient to use.

Figures 9.1 and 9.2 show how a display may look after some typical interactions with a display editor. These figures are anno-

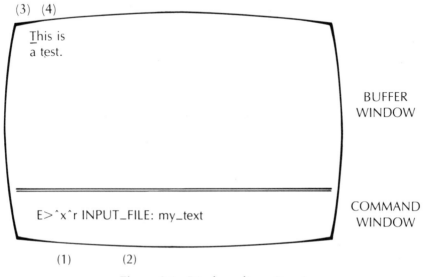

Figure 9.1. Display editor: Part I

Figure 9.2. Display editor: Part II.

tated with numbers in parentheses (outside the "window panes").
The numerical annotations are as follows:

1. The user types a command to read in the contents of a data
    base object to the editor buffer. The editor prompt and
    user command are echoed in the command window.

2. The editor responds by asking the name of the data base
    object. The user types the name (my_text) and terminates
    with a "carriage return."

3. The contents of my_text are read into the buffer and
    displayed in the buffer window.

4. The buffer is marked with a special character (usually
    called a cursor) which helps the user determine which
    changes he will make to his text. Now the cursor is
    displayed at the beginning of the buffer (as the underscore
    character "_").

5. The cursor may be moved by simple commands; text can
    be inserted, deleted, or marked for moving by commands
    based on the cursor position. For example, the command
    "control n" moves the cursor to the next line as shown in
    Figure 9.2. If a command to delete a line is typed, the line
    that the cursor is on will be erased from the display. If the

text "only a little" is typed, the line that the cursor is on will look like this:

only a littlea test

(and the cursor will still be in place).

For many applications, it is convenient to have an editor that "knows" about the language that it has in its buffer. For example, if the language is English, it would be useful if there were simple commands to move letters, words, or paragraphs. For Ada, an editor that was familiar with lexical units, statements, and blocks would similarly be useful. This may be accomplished by setting the editor to a particular "mode." These modes provide the MAPSE user with special commands that take advantage of the syntax of the input language. Sample modes can be

text mode for English syntax;

Ada mode for Ada syntax;

data base mode for pathname syntax;

dumb mode for dumb editor commands (useful if the human only has access to a primitive input device);

normal text mode (with default behavior).

Other tools that frequently are used with the editor are formatting tools. One example seen earlier was an Ada "pretty-printer." These formatting tools have commands of their own that may control indenting, paragraphing, and the placement of comments. A typical formatting tool may involve the creation of a file containing text and format commands; these commands may in fact be all "default" commands. This file is then used as an input parameter to the format tool which creates a new (formatted) file from the input file.

Instead of creating an object, editing it, leaving the editor and calling other tools, we may ask why we have to leave the editor in the first place. If our editor is so convenient to use, why not call the other tools (especially the CLP) from the editor? One might interpret some of the Stoneman guidelines (i.e., integration) as requiring this functionality of our editor.

An editor that accomplishes this is an integrated editor because it is integrated with the rest of the tools. One mechanism that one may see with these integrated editors is that the human can create his own sequence of windows on the display and initiate separate processes inside the windows. Of course, we assume that this mech-

DISPLAY (WINDOW PANES)

(7)	(5)	> get *
M> READ LAST		MAIL_B
FROM: DELUCA		LOG
DATE: 1-APRIL-1985		MY_LIB
SUBJECT: MOVIE		MYPGM
NO. CANT MAKE IT.		MESSAGE

M>_

(1) (2) (4)
(3) > COMPILE MYPGM,

ARRIVE_AT_TABLE;   MYLIB
end DRINK;
end DANCE;   *ЗYNTAX DIAGNOSTIC
end MAIN;   UNKNOWN IDENTIFIER
                      DRING ^o
                      >COMPILE MYPPGM,
                        MYLIB,
                        background

> MAIL_MAN   (6)

Figure 9.3. Integrated editor.

anism provides a way to suspend each process when one changes windows. Integrated editors have the ability to invoke the CLP (and other programs) because they have important access to the KAPSE calling facilities. For similar reasons, they can create and display representations of these processes in a given window and are able to suspend processes (and invoke or spawn other processes) when jumping from window to window.

Figure 9.3 is an annotated display of some typical actions associated with an integrated editor. Four windows (plus a default command window) are displayed; they were constructed as follows:

(a) The window containing (1) is where we begin. The user has just finished editing the Ada program MyPgm. The user now wants to compile it.

(b) The user creates another window (2). This is where compilation is performed. If a trivial syntax error was discovered, the user can jump back to the editing window to correct the error (3), and then jump back to compile (4).

(c) While the program is compiling again, the user creates another Window (5) to look at his directory of files.

(d) The user then creates another Window (6) so he can read his mail (7).

The position of the cursor now has the power of determining what processes the user can command. The job of moving the cursor around (and spawning and aborting processes) can be made easier on the human if a special input device is available. These devices (some of which have names like "light-pen" or "mouse") make such an integrated environment extremely easy to use.

References
The functions of a MAPSE editor are defined in Stoneman [17]. Good surveys on the different kinds of editors available are found in [40]. A transportable Ada tool that has some windowing capability is discussed in [9]. Further observations about Mouses (Mice?) and graphical support are found in [25], [31], and [56].

Problems
1. How can an APSE editor support certain features of the Ada language?

2. What life cycle activities can an APSE editor support?

3. What editor operations are similar to login and logout? Can an editor have the equivalence of login and logout scripts? Why would this be useful?

SECTION THREE
DATA BASE ISSUES

10

What's in a Pathname?

We recall the purpose of the data base according to Stoneman: a data base organizes the information contained in an APSE. In particular, the data base organizes the APSE information that is associated with the storage and configuration management of an Ada programming application. What is included in this information? Everything that pertains to the successful development, delivery, and management of the application. Stoneman says that the data base is "the repository of all information associated with each project throughout the life cycle." The organization of this information is crucial to the Ada applications programmer and to the Ada applications manager. The importance of this organization of project knowledge should not be underestimated. In fact, Stoneman also declares that the data base is "the central feature" of an APSE.

We will examine several aspects of this organization of Ada software life cycle knowledge. We first classify the proper entities in the APSE data base that are needed for APSE software engineering. This classification essentially "types" our data base objects into useful entities that are required by Stoneman but are "independent" of a particular APSE. We will then look at the "internal" aspects of an APSE data base object and see how the Stoneman software engineering concepts correspond with other "Ada" concepts of a pragmatic nature. Finally, we will examine the "external" features of an APSE data base object. These features show how the APSE data base objects are interrelated with each other. Here we will examine one of the most important aspects of the APSE data base: the naming of data base objects.

APSE data base entities are classified by Stoneman into a hierarchy based on management functionality. This hierarchy can also be considered another instantiation of the "layered" model that we see throughout the APSE. Again, this model reflects the principle of abstraction in that a user of the "higher" layers should not worry about the details found in the lower layers. We also recall that this model also promotes sharing. The layers of this model are shown in Figure 10.1. We now examine these layers from the bottom (most specific) layer up.

The entities contained in the lowest layer in our model are called objects. These entities in turn can be classified into files, processes, and devices. These objects have a content that corresponds to what a tool user (human or not) produces as output.

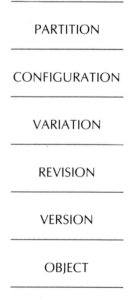

Figure 10.1. APSE data base model.

Tools may produce similar representations of the same object at different times. This abstract grouping of objects is called a version group. This may occur when a human uses his editor to make modifications of a given object containing text. Subsequent editor actions cause the creation of different versions of the "same" text which may be contained in different data base objects. These objects would be distinguished in name by a version number.

Humans may purposely create a similar representation of an object that may correspond to a significant change in the evolution of the application. This frequently happens when errors are found during testing or during maintenance. This conscious human grouping of objects is called a revision group. The application that is delivered to a customer usually corresponds to the latest version of the last revision.

Humans may also purposely create similar representations of objects if this representation corresponds to an instantiation of a generic program unit. For example, a generic Ada package for numerical integration may have several instantiations for several different floating point types. All of these instantiations may be important to some delivered Ada product. One way of managing these instantiations of a generic unit is to create a variation group.

Different objects, versions, revision groups and variation groups may be somehow arbitrarily associated and coupled with each other, especially if these entities are connected with some application. This grouping of data base objects that somehow have the same reason for coexisting is called a configuration.

Before we define the last data base object classification, we must ask one question: Are all APSE users equal? The answer is no. Some APSE users must be responsible for other APSE users. These responsible individuals can be APSE maintainers, Ada program auditors, or Ada applications managers. These people have the power to find out what their APSE users are doing without asking them: they have special access to certain APSE resources. These same people also have the power to provide APSE resources to the people who work for them. As far as they are concerned, it is very convenient to form completely arbitrary groupings of objects, versions, variations, revisions, and configurations without regard to any reason or purpose. These arbitrary groupings are important so that

> people can be assigned particular APSE resoures associated with their jobs,

managers can find out about different Ada applications, and

different sources of information can be "effectively" and arbitrarily organized (which may depend on a particular application or even a particular APSE session).

These "highest-layer" groupings of APSE data are called partitions.

Note that this hierarchy has a certain inheritance property: objects are contained in a version group, a version group may be part of a revision group, this may in turn be part of a variation group which may be part of a configuration. The APSE user of the highest levels also has control of the lowest. A manager can have the power to allocate (or remove) particular partitions of data base objects (resources) to whomever he pleases. Sharing on the higher levels may be achieved if certain "interfaces" are established on the lower levels. These observations imply that we must keep track of who creates the data base object and who uses it. This is important when one wishes to limit the access of knowledge contained in the APSE (or its control). The general principle here is that "knowledge is power" and that power is not to be given away freely. In the APSE, this is especially true because we have real applications with real customers. Disasters can happen too easily if the customer is provided with the wrong information. The APSE mechanism responsible for managing the information controlling interfaces in the APSE data base is called access control.

We now consider the internal model of an APSE data base object. Our goal is to model representations of entities that can be "stored" and whose identities can be binded. In terms of the formal semantics discussed in Section 1, APSE data base entities are also entities of the APSE Store and Environment.

One uniform model of the APSE data base object is the CAIS node model. A node is an entity that has a content, attributes, and relations. Nodes have a set of generic operations associated with them, and may also have a set of auxiliary operations that are defined for their particular node type, which depends on the contents of the node.

The contents of some nodes denote elements that are storable. These nodes (whose content takes on values from the APSE Store domain) are typically called file nodes.

The contents of other nodes denote entities that are bound to some physical device, such as a terminal, a printer, or a tape drive.

These nodes (whose content takes on values from the APSE Environment domain) are typically called device nodes.

The contents of some other nodes are associated with the actual actions of machine computations. These nodes (whose content takes on values from the APSE Continuation domain) are typically called process nodes.

Finally, some nodes are defined to have no content. Like the zero, they denote placeholders in the node model and are used to group other nodes. These nodes are called structure nodes.

All nodes may have relations and attributes. The relations of a node provide information on the behavior of a node with other nodes: relations are a form of "external" or "global" node meta-information. Attributes, on the other hand, provide information on the internal structure of a node: attributes are a form of "internal" or "local" node meta-information.

The node model is a uniform and convenient specification of APSE data base objects that complies with the Stoneman requirements. We now assume the following: A node is a (Stoneman) data base object.

Now, let's investigate how these nodes can be used and manipulated. One requirement is that the node organization mechanism be easy to learn and easy to use. We have seen several times that the traditional organization found in fields as diverse as programming environments and organizational behavior is a tree-like hierarchy. This is very similar to the familiar layered models we have seen before, except that in this case elements of the hierarchy (instances of the layers) are pictured and connected like a tree (with the roots at the top and leaves at the bottom). A particular object in this data base is specified by pointing to where it is in this picture.

The problem that we have is how to develop suitable naming conventions so that elements in the hierarchy can be referred to unambiguously. Figure 10.2 shows one example of such a hierarchy. The lines connecting the nodes represent the relation "reports to," and functionally correspond to interfaces in an OSI-like model. Hence (for example),

Sue reports to Bill.
Sally reports to Bill.
Sam reports to Bill.
Joe reports to Sam.
Jon reports to Sam.

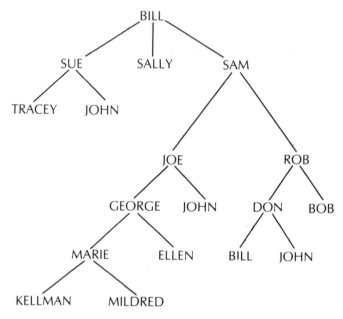

Figure 10.2. Management hierarchy.

There are many useful situations that can be managed with a hierarchical structure. Basically, they can all be distinguished by some relation that has an inheritance or transitive property. One example of such a property is "belongs to." For example, if A belongs to B, and B belongs to C, then A belongs to C. In the organizational chart, this property is observed if we cannot change "report to" to "controls." We can ask questions, like "find all people who are controlled by Sam." In the APSE, this hierarchy can be used to conveniently organize the programs in an Ada application, a sequence of program calls, or a set of APSE users.

There are many useful situations that cannot be managed with a pure hierarchy. One useful situation is to see if we can use our organizational structure to organize a partition that describes all female workers without "knowing in advance" or interrogating each person as to whether he (or she) is a female or not. Other questions of a similar nature come to light. We would (ideally) like associated with each data base object a "personnel file" that contains the following useful information:

who is the object?
what is it and what job does it do?

why is it needed?
who needs it?
when was it created?
how is it used?
where is it in the organization?

We will see later that this can be accomplished by node attributes.

Other examples can be found that show that an hierarchical organization is inadequate. One example can be found in large organizations in which certain individuals sometimes report to managers that do not follow the usual "chain of command." Other individuals may even turn the hierarchy upside-down by being given a job on "special assignment." This is usually shown on an organizational chart by a "dotted line" as in Figure 10.3. Individuals on special assignment frequently have more power than they would otherwise inherit from their position in the hierarchy. Becuse of "special assignments" our tree-like hierarchy may actually correspond to a network.

We will now develop a notation that translates these organizational structures into representations that can be easily understood

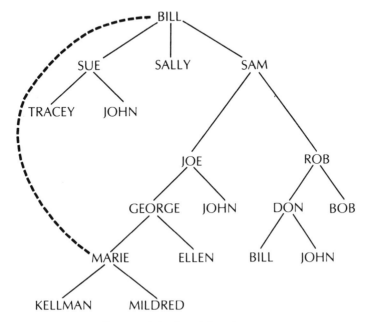

Figure 10.3. Special assignment.

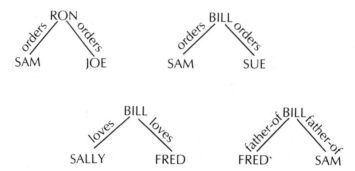

Figure 10.4. Relations and relationships.

and manipulated by an APSE user. In particular, we will develop the important naming conventions that will allow us to locate nodes unambiguously. The solution to our notational problems is found with the key concepts: relations, pathnames and attributes. It will turn out that a node (an APSE data base object) is denoted by a pathname; pathnames are denoted by relations and special attributes.

A relation is a set of node pairs. Each node pair is called a relationship. Examples of relations and relationships are shown in Figure 10.4. The name of one relation is "orders." Each of the following are relationships of the relation whose name is "orders":

> Ron orders Sam.
> Ron orders Joe.
> Bill orders Sue.
> Bill orders Sam.

A relationship is an element of the set of node pairs that defines a relation.

In the figure, Ron orders Sam and Bill orders Sam. One question is if each Sam named in these relationships is the same Sam! We need a convention to specify a node unambiguously.

One method is to identify each node by a distinguishing characteristic. We can assign to each node its unique Social Security number. Consequently, we can refer to this number each time we want to refer to that particular node. (Sometimes this "Social Security number" is called a "node handle.")

One problem with this solution is that we really do not refer to people by their Social Security numbers all the time. We really pre-

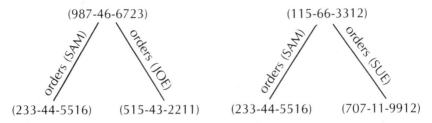

Figure 10.5. Relationship keys and node handles.

fer to call them by name. We can create another naming scheme that reflects this desire by changing our way of naming relations (see Figure 10.5). In this case, we use the "informal" name as a relationship key, and refer to the node by its Social Security number. Actually, since the relation name, the relationship key, and the "source" node of the relation both have a sufficient amount of information to reference the "object" node of the relation, we rarely need to reference the node by the Social Security number. We only have to make sure that one of the nodes is unambiguously specified. Hence, if Bill's number is 987-46-6723, and Sam's is 233-44-5516, then we can interpret the "ambiguous"

"Bill" orders "Sam".

as

987-46-6723 orders Sam.

where we have specified

Node_Handle Relation_Name Relationship_Key

This then denotes the node 233-44-5516.

Relation names and relationship keys can help us unambiguously identify nodes in our organization as long as two requirements are met:

1. We know the identity of the "source" node of a given relation between nodes.

2. The relationship key was chosen correctly. This essentially means that the following function can always be defined:

function Get_Node_Handle (N: Node_Handle;

R: Relation_Name;

K: Relation_Key)

return Node_Handle;

Consequently,

Get_Node_Handle(987-46-6723, Orders, Sam)

evaluates to

233-44-5516

(i.e., the node denoted by Sam)

We now investigate how we can unambiguously name nodes that reside at the "lower ends" of the hierarchy. As long as one "source" node is unambiguously defined, and as long as we meet the above two requirements, then we can unambiguously specify nodes in terms of a sequence of relation names and relationship keys. Such a sequence is called a "pathname." Pathnames may have their own particular syntax. We now examine one syntax of pathname specification.

We assume that our "source" node is the node denoted by Bill (987-46-6723). If we introduce a "predefined" relation name called SOURCE_NODE, another way of saying this could be

'SOURCE_NODE => 987-46-6723

where we use Ada attribute notation. The above attribute expression could be read, "The node denoted by the relation name SOURCE_NODE is specified as the node (handle) 987-46-6723." Given this fact, we can denote the node 233-44-5516 by

'SOURCE_NODE 'ORDERS(SAM)

This can be read as, "The node denoted by the relation called SOURCE_NODE has a relation called ORDERS which, in turn, denotes another node by its relationship key called SAM." This sequence of relation names and relationship keys is called a pathname, since it denotes a "path" through an organizational network: the relation names and relationship keys label the edges of the network (and in turn denote the actual nodes). The actual nodes do not have to be labelled as long as we know the exact identity of the source node. (The actual nodes can always be referenced by their node handles, but this is frequently inconvenient and leaves out much information on "who is who" in our organization.)

Let's introduce some additional terminology to formalize the pathname syntax. An expression of the form

'Relation_Name

or

'Relation_Name (Relationship_Key)

is called a path element. We have seen that these path elements can be used to denote nodes. A sequence of path elements is called a pathname. Pathnames similarly can be used to denote nodes. The only tricky issue associated with interpreting this denotation is that we must unambiguously know our starting "source" node.

There are some pragmatic problems with our notation. We can easily specify objects with pathnames that begin at an unambiguously specified node that we have been calling the "source" node. If we were using our pathname conventions for naming and manipulation of nodes that are (topologically) distant from the source node, frequent manipulation of the data base objects may be tedious and confusing for a human. (If we take the usual network representation of an organization and turn it upside down, the resulting picture looks like a tree. The source node can then be considered a "root" and the distant nodes can be considered "leaves." The problem that we are referring to here is that if we have a rather large tree, a pathname to a particular leaf may be extremely long. These long sequences of pathnames may lead a human into confusion.)

Another potential difficulty may result if we allow more than one source node. This can be seen in Figure 10.5. Ambiguity results in trying to determine which node is to be the SOURCE_NODE in a path element.

One simple way out of these difficulties is to create certain pre-defined relations and functions that can be used to specify "relative" pathnames and "absolute" pathnames.

An absolute pathname avoids the latter type of ambiguity since the convention is made by identifying only one source node. Nodes are defined in terms of a pathname denotation from an unambiguously specified source node that we may call THE_ROOT.

A relative pathname specifies a node in terms of another node that is unambiguously defined. The nodes that are reserved for this purpose are the structure nodes. Creation of a relative pathname is accomplished by the tool

Set_Current_Node(Structure_Node_Denotation = >MySource)

This procedure has the side effect of changing the identity of the source node. The source node (now a structure node) is denoted by the path element

'CURRENT_NODE

For example, in Figure 10.6, if 'CURRENT_NODE initially denotes a structure node Bill, then after the execution of

Set_Current_Node(

'CURRENT_NODE'Orders'(Sam)'Orders(Joe)'Orders(George))

the value of CURRENT_NODE then denotes the structure node denoted by George (122-95-4136). The usefulness of this operation can be seen in how nodes were specified before and after this procedure invocation. For example, before invocation, the node that denotes the person who works for George (122-95-4136) would be denoted by the pathname.

'CURRENT_NODE 'Orders(Sam)'Orders (Joe)'Orders
(George)'Orders(Marie)

After the invocation of the procedure, this node would be denoted by

'CURRENT_NODE'Orders(Marie)

This is shown graphically in Figure 10.6.

We now introduce some conventions that further simplify node denotation through pathname specification. One simplification results from the observation that writing 'CURRENT_NODE before all pathnames does not provide us with any information! As long as we know that all pathnames begin at the 'CURRENT_NODE, and that we have specified this node elsewhere, it is unnecessary to specify it. Consequently, the pathname

'CURRENT_NODE 'Orders(Marie)

can be written as

'Orders(Marie)

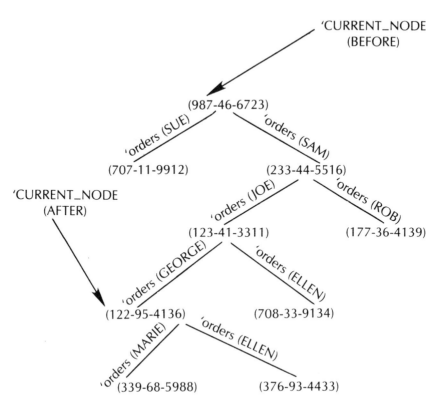

Figure 10.6. Example of Set_Current_Node.

Sometimes (especially when dealing with a management hierarachy), it really is not necessary to specify the relation "Orders." If our particular context is concerned only with the questions of "who orders who" or "who hires who," we should be able to simplify writing pathnames by not having to write " 'Orders " in every path element. This can be accomplished by introducing the concept of a "current" relation. For example, we may have a tool that accomplishes this:

Set_Current_Relation (Relation_Name = > MyDefaultRelation)

To illustrate what this procedure does, we invoke it with

Set_Current_Relation (Orders);

The node specified above by the pathname

'Current_Node'Orders(Sam)'Orders(Joe)'Orders(Sue)'Orders(Marie)

can now be also specified by

Sam.Joe.Sue.Marie

and the value of 'CURRENT_RELATION denotes the relation "Orders". The pathname is simplified; an object is specified only by its relationship keys (provided we know 'CURRENT_NODE and 'CURRENT_RELATION). We note the following conventions, given an arbitrary relationship key we will call Marie:

'CURRENT_RELATION(Marie) abbreviates to

.Marie

'CURRENT_NODE 'CURRENT_RELATION(Marie) abbreviates to

Marie

Sometimes we may also abbreviate 'CURRENT_RELATION to 'DOT as an intermediate translation to the "dot" notation.

We now see how we can handle the situations of "special assignment." To do this we need a name for the "ordinary" pathnames we have been considering. A primary pathname is a pathname that "preserves" the hierarchy of the management organization. A secondary pathname is a pathname that does not preserve the "natural chain of command" order in the management organization. These pathnames may denote objects that illustrate the situation of "special assignment." For example, if Bill wants to form a "special relationship" with Marie (by bypassing the normal "chain of command"), we create the secondary pathname 'Orders(SpecialAssignment) to denote Marie. This may be accomplished by the Link tool. This tool creates another access path to a node by a secondary pathname:

Link (Primary_Pathname = >MySourcePathname,

To_New_Secondary_Pathname = >MyNewPathname);

Consequently, Marie's special assignment with Bill can be indicated by:

Link ('Orders(Sam)'Orders(Joe)'Orders(George)'Orders(Marie),

'Orders(Special Assignment))

If we Set_Current_Relation to Orders, this can also be written as

Link (Sam.Joe.George.Marie, SpecialAssignment)

The pathname SpecialAssignment and the pathname Sam.Joe.George.Marie both denote the same node, namely 339-68-5988. This pathname can be broken with the Unlink tool:

Unlink (SpecialAssignment)

This secondary pathname is shown in Figure 10.7.

So far we have dwelled on the naming mechanism associated with APSE data base objects and nodes. We will now briefly detail some of the tools that can be used to manipulate the contents of these nodes.

The create family of tools creates a node and a primary pathname that puts the node in its proper organizational place. Since we have essentially four types of nodes, we must have four types of node creation tools:

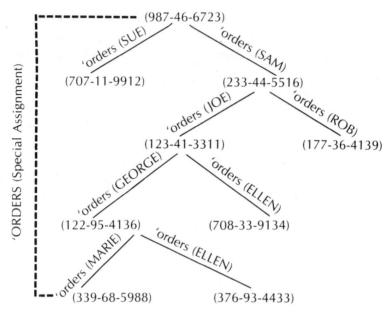

Figure 10.7. A Secondary Pathname.

Create_File (Primary_Pathname = >MyFileName)

Create_Structure (Primary_Pathname = >MyStructureName)

Create_Process (Primary_Pathname = >MyProcessName)

Create_Device (Primary_Pathname = >MyDeviceName)

Another way of parameterizing the create tool is with the following:

Create (Primary_Pathname = >MyNodeName,

    Node_Type = >   MyKindofNode)

where

    type Node_Type is (File, Structure, Process, Device);

The invocation of these tools has the side effect of creating a particular node and a pathname that is bound to that node, together with the default attributes and relations that are appropriate for that node in the context of its creation.

We can similarly dispose of a node (and destroy its primary relationship) with the delete family of tools.

We have seen how A P S E nodes may be named. We now investigate how configurations and partitions of A P S E nodes may be identified so they can be easily accessed. In order to name arbitrary collections of objects, it is convenient to establish some name-matching conventions.

The general principle is that

~ matches any single character in a name
* matches any sequence of characters in a name

We show this mechanism in action with a few examples:

```
get 'Orders(*)    --  Gets the names of all keys associated
                  --  with 'CURRENT_NODE 'Orders.
```

```
get 'CURRENT_NODE'*

                  --  Gets the names of all relation names
                  --  of the current node.
```

```
get *             --  The same as
                  --  get 'CURRENT_NODE'
                  --  CURRENT_RELATION(*)
```

These examples limit themselves to only one level in the hierarchy. A more powerful tool that goes through the entire management organization is the iterate tool:

```
iterate *

                  --  Gets the names of the relations and
                  --  relationship keys of all file nodes
                  --  in the organizational hierarchy,
                  --  starting from 'CURRENT_NODE.
```

```
iterate (Start_Node = >'Orders(Sam),
```

Relation_Name => ~ ~ ~ ~ ,

Keyname =>*,

Node_Type =>Process)

```
--    Gets the names of all relations
--    whose names are constrained to four
--    arbitrary letters, having arbitrary
--    relation name keys,
--    that are bound to process nodes
--    starting from the node 'Orders(Sam)
--    in the hierarchy.
```

Other APSE data bases may have more powerful matching and itera-
tion mechanisms. Some of these facilities may include certain logical
functions associated with attribute and pathname constraints. These
functions may have semantics similar to these Ada reserved
words—not, and, or. Other matching facilities may incorporate a
unifying variable that would "bind" what was being matched. For
example, the unifying variable *X in the following expression

'user(Kell*X)

would match 'User(Kellman), and have the side effect of binding the
variable X to the value "man".

References
APSE data base organizations are described in [4], [5], [6], [8]. The
CAIS node model is described in [15].

Problems
1. How many possible pathnames are there in Figure 10.5?

2. Identify three uses of secondary pathnames in the life cycle of an
   Ada application.

3. A rename tool may exist in some APSES. This tool has the effect
   of changing one pathname into another pathname. Discuss what
   this tool can do to secondary pathnames.

4. Use the iterate tool to find what is in Kellman's data base (in
   Chapter 6).

11

Expressions for Configuration Management

So far, pathnames have roughly told us where a data base object is in a management organization. This information is useful for general project structuring. However, we know there is more to managing a project than "appointing" individuals to fill certain slots (and having these individuals fill other certain slots, and so on). A manager needs a "personnel" department if he is to truly understand what is going on in his departments. Just because a manager knows how to get to different individuals in his organization does not mean that he knows what these individuals are doing, what their background is, and who these individuals communicate with in the organization. The manager may judge an individual's organizational work as far as where he normally fits in the hierarchy (or to whom he reports to in "special assignments"), but this information will not suffice if he does not know which individual is holding crucial information.

In an APSE we have the following equation:

$$\text{configuration management} = \text{pathnames} + \text{attributes}$$

131

Stoneman requires attributes. ("Objects in the data base shall have attributes", according to Stoneman Section 5.A.4). An attribute of an object is "meta-information" that describes the object. This is distinct from the content of an object which is defined as what the object actually contains. One may say that the contents of an object are represented by "raw" information; the contents of the attributes of that same object are represented by certain chunks of relevant knowledge about the object. In the examples of the organizations presented in Chapter 11, some sample attribute names can be SALARY, NEXT_OF_KIN, and WEIGHT. The contents of these attributes may have values such as 37000, "JEFF MICHAELS", and 165.

There are three kinds of attributes that are required to be in an APSE data base: history recording attributes, categorization recording attributes, and access recording attributes.

History recording attributes describe the when, why, and how of an object's creation. We want to record the birthday of the object and who was involved with its birth. A "diary" of the life of the object is also recorded with these attributes.

Categorization recording attributes describe what "kind" of object we have. There are many different "types" of objects associated with the life cycle of an Ada application. Some of these categories of objects may include "Ada source code," "documentation," "testing suite," and so on. Other categorization attributes may simply denote the node type of a particular object (process, structure, file, device).

Access recording attributes specify how we may restrict the use of the knowledge in the data base. Since programs and tools are (declaratively) also represented as data base objects, these attributes may also be used to restrict the use of programs and tools.

One fact emphasized by Stoneman is that these attributes are to be regarded as a "minimal set." The list of possible attribute names should be extensible, just as the list of possible APSE tool names should be extensible. This allows for flexibility. Since Stoneman also specifies that there should be ways to create and manipulate the knowledge in these attributes, many of the tedious details associated with configuration management can be automated by special tools. These configuration management tools make very heavy use of the data base facilities for manipulating attributes.

One simple way of representing the knowledge associated with an object is by an "association list." The set of attributes of an object can be considered to be a table containing the attribute name and the corresponding attribute value. Both of these entities can be implemented with Ada character strings and specially defined procedures for string manipulation.

Different APSEs may have specific attribute naming mechanisms. Some attribute names may be predefined by the APSE and may have contents that can be modified only by special tools. Other attribute names may be predefined but may have contents that can be freely modified. Still other attributes may have names created by a human with special tools.

Let's examine some predefined attributes and see how they may or may not be modified.

The NODE_TYPE attribute essentially "types" our data base objects according to the APSE node model. The contents of this attribute can be PROCESS, STRUCTURE, DEVICE, or FILE.

The CREATION_DATE attribute tells the time and date that the data base object was created.

The DERIVATION_TEXT attribute describes how an object was created. This may include the names of the creating tools (with appropriate parameters) and the names of all other data base objects that were also used in the birth of the object.

The DERIVED_FROM attribute contains the pathnames of the data base objects that were used to create a new data base object. In other words, this attribute records the family tree (of direct ancestors) of a given data base object.

The DERIVES_OTHERS attribute tells how many other data base objects reference this one (in their DERIVED_FROM attribute).

The PURPOSE attribute tells why the data base object exists.

The CONFIGURATION_CONTROL attribute tells if a data base object is under special configuration control. Depending on the APSE, this attribute controls the accounting for the REVISION and VERSION attributes.

The REVISION attribute gives the revision number of an object. Depending on the APSE, REVISION can denote a number or a list of attribute keys.

The MAJOR attribute key gives the number of the major revision.

The MINOR attribute key gives the number of the minor revision.

The VERSION attribute gives the version number of an attribute. Depending on the APSE, VERSION can denote a number or a list of attribute keys.

The BASIS attribute key gives the number of the basis of the version.

The CYCLE attribute key gives the number of the cycle of the version.

The PARENT attribute of an object is the (primary) pathname of the node that was used to establish the creation of the object.

Finally, the attributes that are most used (and abused) are the access control and security control attributes. These are responsible for controlling the use and security of data base objects, and consequently, the APSE tools and programs. As stated above, an APSE user (who may or may not be human) is also defined by a data base object (a pathname). Consequently, the values of these attributes specify which pathnames (users) may or may not have access to resources. Depending on the APSE, the ACCESS_CONTROL attribute may denote a number or a list of attribute keys:

The SECURITY_CONTROL attribute may denote one of several levels of security. These levels can also influence the following ACCESS_CONTROL attributes.

The NO_ACCESS attribute key indicates which pathnames cannot utilize a node (even for the construction of another pathname).

The ACCESS attribute key indicates which pathnames can utilize a node for the construction of pathnames.

The READ attribute key shows which pathnames are able to examine the contents of the data base object.

The APPEND attribute key shows which pathnames can write to the object (from the end).

The WRITE attribute key shows who can manipulate the contents of the object arbitrarily.

The EXECUTE attribute key shows which pathnames can "execute" the object, if it is a tool, a program, or a script.

The CHANGE_ATTRIBUTE attribute key shows which pathnames can change the attributes of the object.

The PATH_NAME attribute key shows which users can use this data base object as a pathname.

Here's a simple example in the use of these attributes. A user named Kellman wishes to protect a data base object of NODE_TYPE file. (We assume that CURRENT_NODE is 'USER(Kellman).) He then does the following:

>create (marie, node_type = > file)

-- This creates a file node and assigns to it the APSE default
-- attributes.

> set marie'access_control (no-access = >'user(*),

read = > "")

Kellman created a file called "marie" (which has a pathname from the 'CURRENT_NODE as 'USER(KELLMAN).MARIE). He then wishes to give it the highest protection. He specified that no other nodes denoted by the user relation name can access it, and that no one (denoted by the null string) can read it. Unfortunately, these two specifications include 'user (kellman) himself. Kellman cannot use the name marie in a pathname, nor can he read the contents of the file marie.

Let's see the contents of the default attributes of the object marie before Kellman changed them. This is accomplished if the following was typed before the set command:

>list marie'*

CATEGORY   = >FILE

CREATION_DATE   = >1-APRIL-1985-11:05:33

DERIVATION_TEXT   = >CREATE

DERIVED_FROM   = >""""

DERIVES_OTHERS   =>''''   --   empty

PURPOSE   =>''''   --   no purpose given by
                                          --   Kellman

CONFIGURATION_CONTROL   =>YES

REVISION   =>(MAJOR=>0,

                                   MINOR=>0)

VERSION   =>(BASIS=>0,

                                   CYCLE=>0)

PARENT   =>'USER(KELLMAN)

NO_ACCESS   =>''''   --   all users have access

READ   =>'USER(*)

WRITE   =>'USER(KELLMAN)

APPEND   =>'USER(KELLMAN)

EXECUTE   =>''''   --   This is not executable.

PATHNAME   =>''''   --   This is not a structure.

CHANGE_ATTRIBUTE   =>'USER(KELLMAN)

SECURITY_CONTROL   =>UNCLASSIFIED

Note how we made use of partitions to specify "families" of pathnames (i.e., arbitrary groupings of objects). There are other ways that we can specify these pathnames for our access attributes. One other way uses the concept of roles.

Suppose an APSE project manager has the power to tell people what to do. Therefore, this manager has the power to assign roles. To assign these roles, he may have access to some special APSE tools. For this example, we assume that the manager is in charge of a relation name called

'PROJECT

and that he makes the following roles for this pathname:

role (name => reviewer,

        access => read)

role(name => tester,

        access => read, execute)

role(name => programmer,

        access => read, write, execute)

The individuals who work on this project may now be given identities by this manager who is in charge of this project:

set_role(user_path_name => 'user(kellman),

    role   => reviewer)

set_role (user_path_name => 'user(mattarrazzo),

    role   => programmer)

When the manager creates relative pathnames at the 'project base node, access to data base objects are given in terms of the roles that particular users play.

How do APSE users manipulate attributes? How do they create their own attributes? Kellman may wish to create his own attribute and provide it with a default value with the set tool:

>   set marie'rating, 10

He may check if an object has a particular attribute with the get tool and list its contents with the list tool:

>get marie'rating

    YES

>list marie'rating

MARIE'RATING = > 10

He may also use the values of attributes in assignments:

> set x list marie'rating

> list x

10

Finally, he may delete the attributes that he defined:

> delete marie'rating

> get marie'rating

NO   --   There is no attribute called rating.

We conclude by examining the other requirements that Stoneman states: the ability to make and manipulate versions, variations, revisions, and partitions. One way is by using the create tool:

> create (shuttle,node_type = >structure)

    --   This builds a node that can be used as a
    --   conventional directory.
    --   A file can be created (with configuration
    --   control default values) by

> create (shuttle.radar, file)

    --   The following invocation

> create shuttle.radar'revision(major = >23,minor = >112),

        'version(basis = >21,cycle = >5)

would create the fifth cycle of the twenty-first basis of the one-hundred and twelfth minor revision of the twenty-third major revision of the file shuttle.radar.

Other APSEs may have other tools that may aid in the configuration management of large projects. Here is an example of the composite tool:

>   composite(name = >shuttle,

            relation = > module,

                       version,

                       revision)

We can construct objects through pathnames:

>   create (shuttle'module(radar)'revision(1)'version(1), file)

Relation names of composites can be assigned arbitrarily (it assumes that the APSE user knows what he is doing). We can use this tool to make variations:

>   composite(trigonometry,

            relations = > variation, version, revision)

>   create (trigonometry'variation(real),

                       'version(1),

                       'revision(1),

                       node_type = >file)

>   create (trigonometry'variation(integer),

                       'version(1)'revision(1),

                       file)

139

This makes two files for trigonometry: one file for "real" operations and one for "integer" operations. We say that these files form variations of each other.

There may be other special purpose tools that manipulate revisions and versions. These and other tools that may affect configuration management may in turn be inhibited from their actions by a lock tool.

References
The tools and attributes discussed here can be found in [4], [5], [6], [8], [10], [11], [13], [14], [15], [17], [32], [33], [46].

Problems
1. Discuss the differences between revisions, variations, and versions.

2. How may these attributes be implemented in your favorite programming support environment?

3. Help user Kellman protect his file correctly by showing which attributes he should have used.

4. Discuss the potential ambiguity in using the same notation for both pathnames and attributes. How can the ambiguity be avoided in the overloaded tool names?

12

Library Tools

What is a program library? Program libraries contain compilation units, support the Ada separate compilation mechanism, and also support the Ada compilation rules. More concretely, program libraries contain the output of tools like compilers and linkers. Program libraries do not contain Ada source programs or files of executable machine instructions. However, a program library is associated with one and only one target.

In an APSE, program libraries occupy the same place as the private types in the Ada language. Program libraries are protected. APSE users cannot edit them, write to them, or explicitly append to them. This can be done indirectly by special tools (such as the compiler). However APSE users do have special library tools available to them so they can find out about their libraries. We can consider the Ada program library to correspond to the private type in the following package:

```
generic

    type Target is (<>);

package Ada_Programming is

    type Program_Library is private;

    procedure Compile (L: in out Program_Library;

                        S: Ada_Compilation_Unit);

    procedure Link (L: in out Program_Library;

                    C: Compiled_Units);

    package Library_Tools is

            --   Tools that modify objects of type

            --   Program_Library

    end Library_Tools;

    --   Other APSE tools.

end Ada_Programming;
```

Where does an APSE user's library reside? APSE libraries are denoted by a pathname just like any other data base object. A library contains library files; consequently, the library is of node_type structure. However, the library cannot be part of a pathname (it has a restricted PATHNAME attribute).

There are several files associated with program libraries. An APSE user does not have access to the contents of these files, but he does have access to their attributes. These library files correspond to the specification and body parts of Ada compilation units, the specification and body parts of (separately compiled) Ada subunits, and files that represent linked compilation units. These files are protected, and are associated with the predefined attributes discussed earlier. There may be several attributes predefined for these library files. They are

TARGET

DEPENDS_ON

REFERENCED_BY

These attributes can be examined and modified by the subcommands in the special interactive library tool. We can also create libraries with the create subcommand, delete library files (or entire libraries) with the delete subcommand, get the names of the files in the library with the get subcommand, and list the contents of the attributes of the library files with the list subcommand. We may also archive (and unarchive) libraries to an external storage medium.

The contents of the library files can be changed by the compiler, assembler, linker, exporter, and importer. In general, when these tools change the library files, these files either become revised (a new version is created and the old one saved), or the changed file overwrites the latest version (so no old version is kept). We now briefly summarize the effects of these tools on an APSE library.

An Ada compiler is given an Ada compilation unit to translate into machine language. The resultant translation is placed in a library file.

An assembler is given an assembly language program to translate into machine language. The resultant translation is placed in a library file.

A linker is given various machine representations of an Ada program (the outputs of an Ada compiler or an assembler, together with other support programs) and produces a set of machine instructions that can be executed by the target. The resultant entity is placed in a library file.

An exporter takes the executable representation of an Ada program from a program library file and places it into a target object prior to its execution.

An importer takes a set of machine instructions (that was the result of another language translation) and places it into a library file (so it can be used by the linker).

The files associated with a program library denote the names of Ada compilation units. The separate compilation facilities of Ada also imply that the library file pathnames may also denote subunits. The library must account for the specification and body parts of library units, for the body parts of subunits (separately compiled bodies), and for linked units. Certain distributed programming tools also reveal that the library should also account for the specification parts of subunits (we will see this in Chapter 17).

One naming mechanism uses the following naming formats for library files:

compilation_unit_name'spec

compilation_unit_name'body

compilation_unit_name'subunit_name'spec

compilation_unit_name'subunit_name'body

linked_unit_name

These pathnames for the library files assume that the particular library structure is the 'CURRENT_NODE.

Library files are also always under configuration control and are protected but may have the following attributes that can be examined:

NODE_TYPE

CREATION_DATE

DERIVATION_TEXT

DERIVED_FROM

DERIVES_OTHERS

VERSION

REVISION

ACCESS_CONTROL

SECURITY_CONTROL

TARGET

DEPENDS_ON

We now examine the effect of a user-invoked tool on the library files with regard to a simple configuration control mechanism. Suppose MY_LIB is a library. In 'USER(KELLMANN), the file SPEC contains the specification part of an Ada compilation unit, and the file BODY contains the body part of the same Ada compilation unit.

> compile spec,my_lib

-- This creates A'SPEC'VERSION(1) in MY_LIB

> compile body,my_lib

-- This creates A'BODY'VERSION(1) in MY_LIB

> compile spec,my_lib

-- A recompilation of spec. Was the old version of spec
-- used for anything? Does anything depend on the previously
-- compiled specification of A? Yes, of course:
-- A'body'version(1).
-- Consequently, A'SPEC'VERSION(2) is created in MY_LIB.

> compile body,my_lib

-- Was A'body'version(1) used in any derivation? No.
-- Consequently, a new
-- A'BODY'VERSION(1) is created that overwrites the old one.

The attributes of the library files that we have created can be examined and created only with the library tool. After invoking the library tool with

> library

L> set_current_node my_lib

-- This could also have been achieved by invoking the library
-- tool with my_lib as an argument.

We can create and delete a library and examine the contents of library file attributes. For example:

    L>   list a'spec'creation_date

            14-January-1985

    L>   set a'body'access_control(access = >'user(kellman),

                        'user(marie)   )

    L>   get a'body'n*

                NODE_TYPE   --   The only attribute that matches.

    L>   list a'body'node_type

            FILE

    L>   set_current_node 'user(kellman)

        --   Go back to the top level of the library.

    L>   delete ex_lib   --   Delete the contents of a library ex_lib.

    L>   set_current_node other_lib

            --   Other library actions.

    L>   exit   --   The 'CURRENT_NODE is set to whatever it was when
                --   the library tool was invoked (in this case,
                --   'user(kellman)   ).

We will examine the tools that affect the library files in much greater detail in Section 4.

References
The nature of the Ada program library is discussed in Stoneman [17]. The library file naming conventions presented here are similar to [5].

Problems

1. What are the advantages and disadvantages of protecting library files?

2. What are the advantages and disadvantages of having a special library tool that manages the library files?

3. What are the advantages of automatically controlling the version numbers of library files?

13

Help!
What Does This
Tool Do?

Stoneman requires the APSE to be easy to learn and easy to use. One way of making this possible is to provide adequate help facilities that are also easy to learn and use. These help facilities should be available to the APSE user at all times.

What do these help facilities include? At any given state of the APSE, these facilities may provide the APSE user with:

parameter options (what actions are presently available);

parameter defaults (how an abbreviation may be filled in);

a short description (what a given APSE resource is supposed to do);

a short example (how a given APSE resource is supposed to be used);

a reference to more extensive documentation.

How are the help facilities used by a human A P S E user? Essentially it depends on the C L P. The C L P model that we have been using assumes that an M C L sequence of command patterns are identified and intelligently parsed. Some of these patterns may denote commands to the help tool. Other patterns denote the other M C L actions discussed in Section 2. If any pattern in this sequence cannot be recognized (or if an error is recognized), a suitable message is displayed to the human.

Some basic help patterns that can be recognized by the C L P include

? , which lists a set of options and names of parameters, and

$, which fills in abbreviations

For more detailed help, the A P S E user is encouraged to use the interactive help tool called "help".

>help

-- The human calls help tool from C L P.

H> -- the help tool prompt

H> ? -- the human needs help on everything: after this is
-- recognized, help responds with a large list:

GET	SET	LIST	CREATE
COPY	COMPARE	DESCRIBE	DEBUG
DELETE	EDIT	EXPORT	IMPORT
LIBRARY	EXAMPLE	ARCHIVE	RETRIEVE
ASSEMBLE	COMPILE	PUT	PRINT
LOCK	UNLOCK	HELP	SEPARATE

^o   -- and so on . . .

There are two important subcommands in the help tool. DE-SCRIBE provides a short description of an APSE resource, its purpose, and why a user would use it. EXAMPLE provides a short example on how the tool would be used as far as the correct syntax and semantics are concerned. Here are some examples:

H> describe compile

Compile translates the Ada source program contained in one or more Ada compilation units. It then generates a sequence of machine instructions for a target. The compilation units are contained in the library that is given to COMPILE. The target machine is indicated by the TARGET attribute of the library ^o. . . .

H>describe link

Link binds the different library file objects and consolidates them into a library file object whose name is supplied by the tool user. This tool distinguishes the main Ada program by a parameter in its option list. Run time support libraries are also linked into this library object. The target machine is indicated by the TARGET attribute of the library ^o . . . .

H>describe export

Export transforms a linked object from the given library into the suitable target format that is necessary for target execution. Debugging kernals may be optionally ^o. . . .

H> describe archive

ARCHIVE takes a specified list of data base objects that are to be saved for long term storage. The archive tool will prompt you for the name of a pathname that denotes a file, partition or configuration that is to be saved or retrieved, or whose ARCHIVE status is to be examined.

H>describe assemble

Assemble produces a machine language program from a file node that contains assembler language. This machine language program is placed in a library file of the specified library. The assembler language and target machine must be ^o. . . .

H>describe export

Export transforms a linked object from the library (see linker) into a format that is necessary for target execution. Debugging kernals may be optionally specified ^o. . . .

H>describe lock
> Lock makes the last version or revision of a node unchangeable Lock is used with configuration ˆo. . . .

H>describe import
> Import is used to input computer programs that have been compiled by the specified compiler into an APSE program library. These imported machine language programs can then be used by the linker to link an Ada package that has been compiled with the Interface pragma ˆo. . . .

H>describe print
> Print takes the contents of a specified node and places it on the printer queue so it can be printed ˆo. . . .

H>describe separate
> Separate creates a separate library file for each Ada task that is to execute on a single target. This tool separates the task from the specified program library and places it into the detached program library. Both libraries must have equal target attributes because ˆo. . . .

H>describe generate_stub
> Generate_Stub creates an Ada subprogram or package body alias (called a stub). The Ada subprogram and Ada package body can then be linked by the linker. The effect of the stub is to insert calls to TEXT_IO to print out the name of the body when it is referenced ˆo. . . .

Since the help tool is an APSE tool, it is subject to the same criteria as other APSE tools. In particular, its input and output may be redirected.

References
Examples of tools with good help facilities are in[41] and [47]. Some advanced help facilities (especially the Do What I Mean, or DWIM tool) are described in [50].

Problems
1. Would it be a good idea to provide an "undo" command or prefix that would "undo" the actions that were performed by an

APSE user? Describe the pros and cons of the following undo commands: unarchive, unedit, uncompile, unseparate, undelete.

2. What may happen if an APSE user is interacting with his APSE on a network, where the special help patterns are actually special instructions to the network switch? Use the set command and some of the results in Section 2 to fix this.

Section Four
Runtime Support

14

What is Runtime Support?

R untime support refers to the set of library facilities that is supplied with an APSE that directly supports the execution of Ada programs on an intended target. This support is highly dependent on the nature of the target, and is meant to help map the meanings of Ada programs into the meanings associated with executing a sequence of target machine instructions. This mapping cannot be accomplished by a simple translation process alone. Ada leaves out many meanings that a translator would have to know. (We saw the many pragmatic details and "undefinitions" that the Ada LRM does not specify in Section 1.) Consequently, we will see that there is more to translating Ada programs into machine instructions than meets the eye.

Runtime support is concerned with the actual environment in which the target Ada program executes. Essentially, this support is concerned with several details of management:

memory management
control management
binding management

Memory management refers to the target mechanism responsible for functions like loading data into memory (paging). Control management includes functions like exception handling and task scheduling. Finally, binding management provides a mechanism for keeping track of names and addresses (especially those names and addresses associated with devices or entry call interrupts).

We can examine these target functions in the context of formal semantics. Just as we considered the semantic domains for Ada programs, we may consider the semantic domains for machine language programs. Memory management can be specified by the target Store domains; control management can be specified by the target Continuation domains; and binding management can be specified by the target Environment domains. Our goal is to build the correspondance between the domains of meanings for Ada programs and the domains of meanings for machine instructions. We want to show that the meanings denoted by Ada programs and the meanings denoted by compiled Ada programs match. This matching function essentially specifies the operational semantics of the Ada program, as shown in Figure 14.1.

Also, just as there are various support mechanisms for the Ada program on the host, there are various Ada support mechanisms for Ada programs on the target. These support mechanisms depend strongly on the capability of the target. However, if we consider that the semantic domains of the target are identical to the semantic domains of the host, then we note (neglecting pragmatic concerns) that any Ada program that can execute on the host can execute on the target. This would also presumably include the entire APSE! The only crucial differences between host and target are the pragmatic differences related to memory size and speed of the computer.

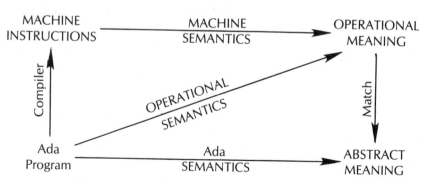

Figure 14.1. Ada program operational semantics.

What areas are especially critical for run time support? The basic areas are tasking, exception handling, and program invocation. From the top down, runtime support is concerned with the following questions:

How are the Ada programs transformed into sequences of machine instructions?

What is necessary for this transformation so that the target instruction sequence will have the same meaning as the original Ada program?

What is the target machine actually capable of in an operating environment, especially in regard to memory, control, and bindings?

How is a transformed Ada program placed into the target and commanded to execute?

How are Ada tasking semantics actually realized in the operating environment of the target?

How do the predefined library packages (for example: package CALENDAR, package SYSTEM, and package TEXT_IO) become associated with a target Ada program?

A brief answer to the last question will serve as an introduction to the remaining sections. A given Ada program can be translated into a sequence of machine instructions by executing a number of tools (which are also programs written in Ada) with our given Ada program as input. A tool called the compiler does the bulk of the work. However, the output of the compiler (a sequence of machine instructions) cannot be executed on the target just yet. First, separately compiled units (from our original Ada program and from the predefined library packages) must be consolidated. This is done by a tool called the linker. Can the output of the linker (another sequence of machine instructions) be executed? Again, not just yet. This output must be correctly formatted so that the target machine will know what to do with it. Also, depending on the target, this sequence of machine instructions (corresponding to our original Ada program) may have to be appended to a special predefined list of target instructions so that the target can handle the special actions requested by our Ada Program. The tool that does this job is called the exporter. Finally, this program can be executed on the target and its actions assessed. This sequence of semantic transformations is summarized in Figure 14.2.

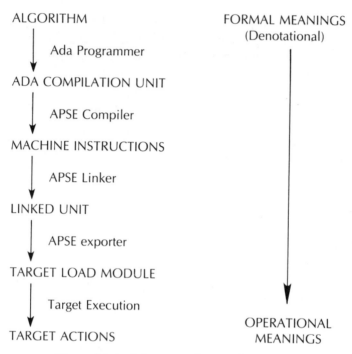

Figure 14.2. Ada semantic transformations.

We must be very specific on the nature of the target. The target computer does not refer to the target "hardware" only: a target computer is specified uniquely by its hardware (instruction set architecture) and its operating system, if one is indeed supplied. So, for example, given the ZONK-11 computer, the following form three target configurations:

1. The ZONK-11 with no operating system (a "bare" ZONK-11).

2. The ZONK-11 running the iSCREAM operating system.

3. The ZONK-11 running the uSCREAM operating system.

Of course, a compiler writer may want to take advantage of the similarities between the iSCREAM and uSCREAM operating systems. However, to the APSE user and Ada applications developer, these targets should be considered distinct.

You may observe that these runtime issues are really binding issues: we are binding meanings. These meanings that we bind are of the following form:

Who in the Ada Program ————> Who in the target

We now look at these issues and how the APSE helps to resolve them.

References
Definitions of APSE runtime support are found in [4] and [17]. A good reference that shows the correspondance between operational and denotational approaches to semantics is [53].

Problems
1. An Ada compiler is not required to implement the predefined input-output packages. Discuss how this may affect compiler writers and APSE users.

2. What are the advantages and disadvantages of considering the *same computer* with a *different operating* system as a *different target?*

15

Runtime
Support Tools

Let's now examine those tools whose use is necessary during the implementation stage of the life cycle of an Ada application. The tools that we will exmaine here are the compiler, the linker, the importer and the exporter.

Here are some typical ways that an APSE user may invoke the APSE compiler:

>compile(source_file = >my_ spec,

library = >my_lib)

>compile my_spec, my_lib

>compile (my_spec, my_lib,

options = >nil)

>compile my_spec, my_lib,

options = >(source = >yes, xref = >no,
private = >yes)

However, these are not the only parameters to the compiler. Some options and their defaults are:

source_file: The pathname of the file that contains the Ada source text containing one or more Ada compilation units that are to be compiled.

library: The name of the library where the compiled units will be placed.

option_list: These include:
listing: This tells the compiler to produce a listing (formatted and numbered)of the Ada source text. In our example, this listing will be contained (depending on the particular APSE configuration management) in the node my_spec'listing'version(1). The default is NO.

private: This tells the compiler to list the private part of the package specifications in the above listing. The default is YES.

xref: This tells the compiler to produce a cross-reference table. This listing is contained (in our example) in the file my_spec_'xref'version(1). The default is NO.

statistics: This tells the compiler to produce a list of how many Ada syntax categories were used. In our example, the listing is contained in the file my_spec'statistics'version(1). The default is NO.

machine: This tells the compiler to list the actual sequence of machine instructions of the compiled unit. This listing is available for inspection only (it cannot be executed). In our example, this listing is contained in the file my_spec'machine'version(1). The default is NO.

diagnostics: This tells the compiler to produce a text of detailed compiler messages and diagnostics for the compilation. In our example, this listing is appended to the file called Message. The default is YES.

optimize: This tells the compiler to optimize according to the source pragmas that have been inserted into the submitted Ada compilation unit. The default is NO.

frequency: This tells the compiler to insert "hooks" to monitor how often an Ada block is entered and executed when it is running on the target. The default is NO.

timing: This tells the compiler to insert "hooks" to monitor the amount of time an Ada block is taking when it is executing on the target. The default is NO.

debug: This tells the compiler to insert "hooks" that will enable the debug tool to dynamically monitor the execution of an Ada program on the target. The default is NO.

What do some of these listings look like? Suppose we create a new file called Pgm that has the following Ada text as contents:

with Text_io; procedure R is

    X: CONSTANT STRING   := "HELLO";

BEGIN TEXT_IO.PUT(X); END;

Figures 15.1, 15.2, and 15.3 show the contents of the files Pgm'listing'version(1), Pgm'xref'version(1), and Pgm'statistics'version(1). Depending on the particular APSE, different compiler listings will contain more or less information and will be subject to different configuration management criteria.

    Besides all these optional listings, what does the compiler actu-

Line	Block	Statement Number
1	1	1: with TEXT_IO;
1	1	2: procedure R is
2	1	3: x: constant STRING: = "HELLO";
3	1	4: begin
3	1	5: TEXT_IO put (X);
3	1	6: end;

Figure 15.1. Contents of Pgm'listing'version(1).

Name	Statement Number	Block Level	Scope	Type
R	2	1	R SET: 2 USED:	procedure
X	3	1	R SET: 3 USED: 5	STRING

Figure 15.2. Contents of Pgm'xref'version(1).

Category	Number	Line
Compilation_UNIT	1	1
Subprogram_declaration	1	2
Object_declaration	1	3
Subprogram_call	1	5
Assignment_statement	1	3

'USER (Kellman)
LIBRARY => MY_LIB
DATE => 1-APRIL-1985
STORAGE_UNITS => 763

STATEMENTS	6
COMMENTS	0
LINES	6
LEXICAL ELEMENTS	12

Figure 15.3. Contents of Pgm'statistics'version(1).

ally create? The compiler creates library files. As we have previously seen, these files cannot be directly modified by the APSE user and contain important information that supports the Ada separate compilation mechanisms as well as the target runtime systems. Remember, when an APSE user creates a program library with the LIBRARY tool, he must specify a target. Library files normally contain:

history and derivation attributes, especially the pathnames of the Ada source files that derived the library file;

intermediate machine code (corresponding to the Ada abstract syntax and frequently specified in DIANA, as specified in Section 1) to keep track of the compiled units, library units referenced in Ada WITH clauses, generic instantiations, and other information about statements, expressions, and identifiers;

a table of Ada lexical units that the program uses;

a list of target dependent statements, expressions, and addresses;

an intermediate sequence of unformatted target machine instructions;

a sequence of formatted machine instructions with external names, addresses, and relocation information that is needed to link and export the target program onto the target;

"hooks" for special runtime tools (like timing analyzers and debuggers) that help monitor the execution of the target program;

optimization information (when requested);

statistics, cross-references, diagnostic information, and compilation units listings (when requested).

Most of the library files indicated above are totally inaccessible to the APSE user (but would be available to the APSE tool builder).

The compiler has a lot of work to do. We also note that the Ada compiler does not only "compile" Ada: it also knows what to do with Ada programs with machine code insertions. Finally, we note that several of these compiler options may depend on some predefined (or implementation dependent) pragmas. These pragmas and options may influence the pragmatics of Ada as well as the runtime behavior of our Ada target program.

An APSE compiler supports the Ada language during the implementation stage of the Ada application life cycle. However, as we observed in Section 1, the APSE must also provide integrated support to other aspects of the life cycle of the Ada application. In particular, the APSE must support those features of the Ada language that support modern software engineering practice. These features are supported implicitly in Ada. (The LRM refers to this implicit support by using the word "permit.")

Let's now discuss what software engineering practices are permitted by Ada in the context of runtime support.

Ada permits hierarchical program development with the use and construction of separately compiled units. In particular, we should be able to compile and execute an Ada program with "missing" bodies (to be supplied later as separately compiled units). This method of program development, called incomplete programming, is useful for separately building and validating different Ada program units. The APSE should support incomplete programming.

Ada permits implementations to interface with other languages, providing that one follows the LRM guidelines in the use of the interface pragma. In particular, an Ada program that uses a package compiled with a pragma interface as its body should be able to be compiled and executed. The APSE should support the uses of the interface pragma if it is desireable to utilize programs written in other languages.

Ada permits task execution to be considered as if tasks were either executing on one (time-shared) target machine or on one task per target machine. In particular, we should be able to compile and execute an Ada program that is to run on more than one target machine. The APSE should support the necessary mechanisms that can enable an Ada program to be distributed across targets. This situation is frequently referred to as distributed programming.

Part of the life cycle support for an Ada application includes the support for certain mechanisms that enable an Ada applications programmer to verify or validate the program with respect to its specifications. This activity is frequently called "quality assurance." One aspect of quality assurance is concerned with carefully examining a program (frequently by interactive testing) with the intention of surfacing potential errors. These errors are then "removed" once they are discovered. The activity of finding and removing such errors is made more productive by the utilization of special purpose tools. Many years ago, when these tools were not available, this activity was very tedious for a human. The tediousness gave this important activity a somewhat unfortunate name: debugging. Fortunately, the APSE provides support for debugging tools and support for other tools related to quality assurance.

Let's summarize the translation actions of the compiler. The

168

Ada compiler translates an Ada compilation unit into a sequence of machine instructions. The compiler inserts the appropriate calls to other library units that are mentioned in WITH clauses. The compiler inserts the appropriate calls to other predefined packages as well as to a special target-dependent runtime support library package. These packages are not normally accessible to the APSE user: they are separately compiled for the target machine indicated by the TARGET attribute of the library.

Now, where is the actual sequence of machine instructions inserted in the place of all these calls?

The answer is in the special tool called the APSE linker. Let's see how the linker is used in supporting the target execution of an Ada application.

The linker is responsible for the following actions:

The linker combines separately compiled units into an entity called a "linked unit." Externally referenced names are matched with the sequence of machine instructions that they actually denote.

The linker combines runtime support units (from a particular runtime library associated with the target) into the linked unit. The calls to the runtime support units were inserted by the compiler.

The linker designates one named program as the "main" program. This program will recieve initial control when the linked unit is executed on the target.

The linker can designate programs as remote target tasks. These programs are separated Ada tasks whose execution is governed by Ada task semantics. If requested, a special topology specification that helps organize the allocation of task objects can be supplied.

The linker allocates storage space to the sequence of target machine instructions and also to the data required by these instructions. If requested, a special overlay specification that helps organize the target memory can be supplied.

The linker checks all units for compliance to the Ada compilation rules. Listings that show how these units are linked together are created.

Here are some typical MCL linker invocations:

```
>link (main_program = >my_main, linked_unit = >my_link,

     library = >my_lib)

>link my_main, my_link,my_lib

>link (my_main, my_lib, my_link,

     options = >(symbol = >YES))
```

As with the compiler, there are several parameters and options that may be supplied:

main_program: the name of either (a) a "main" program, (b) null, if we do not want any main program, or (c) remote, if the library contains a task that is to be placed on a target different from that of the "main" program.

output: the name of the linked unit that the linker will create and place in the library.

library: the name of the program library that contains the compilation units to be linked as well as the linked unit that the linker creates.

options can be chosen from:

symbol: produces the file name'linked that contains a list of names that the linker knows about. (The default is NO)

unit: produces the file name'unit that contains the following information for each linked object: (a) the size of the machine instructions and machine data, (b) the compilation date, (c) history and diagnostic information. (The default is NO)

overlay: specifies the name of a file that contains an overlay specification (in a particular notation) for target memory allocation. (The default is null, which denotes that no user specified memory allocation is needed for the target.)

topology: specifies the name of a file that contains a topology specification (in a particular notation) for target process allocation. (The default is null, which denotes that no user specified process allocation is needed for the target.)

The linker is crucial for the transformation of an Ada program into an executing process. The linker determines how process storage is to be allocated: for some APSE targets, the user may help specify the storage required for each process on the target with an overlay specification. The linker also determines how processes are allocated: for some APSE targets, the user may help specify the target required for each process with a topology specification. We will discuss some aspects of this specification in Chapter 17.

Another facility that concerns the APSE linker is "imported" programming. The APSE linker knows what to do with programs in a foreign language. However, before these programs can be linked, they must be processed by the importing tool.

We illustrate this with an example. Suppose we wish to use a collection of FORTRAN programs that belong to a FORTRAN mathematical subroutine library called MSL. This library has also been compiled by the FORTRAN compiler which produced the sequence of machine instructions for one of our APSE targets. What must we do to use this FORTRAN library?

1. Write a special package specification for this FORTRAN library in Ada. This is discussed in Section 13.9, LRM:

package MSL is

    function ORANG(X:Float)return Float;

    function ATAN(X:Float)return Float;

    -- and so on

private

    pragma Interface (FORTRAN,ORANG);

    pragma Interface (FORTRAN,ATAN);

--

end FortranLib;

2. Compile this package specification into your program library. This creates the library file FortranLib'spec.

3. We must now get the output of the FORTRAN compiler into our library, associated with the package body for MSL:

    3.1.1 Get this object off a storage device (such as magnetic disk, paper tape, or punched cards) and read this into an APSE data base object. We assume that our APSE has the appropriate facilities for retrieving data from external storage devices (these are necessary in order to share resources across APSES). We denote this APSE object that contains the output of the Fortran compiler as MSL_FORTRAN.

    3.2. Use the importer tool:

    import(source_file => MSL_FORTRAN,

    library_file => my_lib,

    specification => FortranLib)

    We have now created a "compilation unit" out of the "body" MSL_FORTRAN (the compiled FORTRAN library). The library file created by the importer is FortranLib'body.

4. We now link the program library with our main program and proceed with our application.

There are several problems associated with imported programs. We can observe these problems even in our simple example above. First, which FORTRAN is specified? The "output of the FORTRAN compiler" can possibly denote hundreds of dialects. Second, we observe that we must be extremely careful in writing a "special package specification" for the FORTRAN subroutine library. A particular problem is concerned with the different parameter passing mechanisms between Ada and FORTRAN. How would we handle a FORTRAN EXTERNAL parameter? Would we have to treat all parameters as Ada in our parameters, or can we get around all this by some special APSE "side effect" mechanism (that may not be clear to the reader of the program, but would provide the intended support). Finally, we observe that the APSE was meant to fully support Ada application programs and not FORTRAN programs. Stoneman did not specify a FAPSE. An APSE that includes a high degree of bilingual support must address these and similar problems.

We still have some outstanding problems to answer that surfaced when we discussed the compiler. Even after compiling and linking, our transformed Ada program is still not in the correct target format for it to be executed. We must use the exporter tool to transform our linked unit into the correct target format before we are able to run our program.

The exporter converts the linked Ada program into a particular format for the target. This formatted entity is sometimes called a target load module, or TLM. The exporter also generates a "runtime kernel" (the Target Ada Support Kernel, or TASK) for each specified target. This TASK is necessary for handling task and memory management (like scheduling and paging), exception propagation, and input-output devices. The TASK is appended to the TLM and placed in an APSE data base object. This file can be

(a) executed on the host, if the host was the target for our Ada program, or
(b) written to a tape, loaded onto the target, and executed on the target.

Here are some typical MCL invocations of the exporter:

>export(linked_object = >my_link,

    library = >my_lib,

    output_file = >my_exe)

>export my_link,my_lib,

    options = >(frequency = >yes, timing = >yes, debug = >yes)

173

The options to the exporter deal with the insertion of different "support kernels" associated with different analysis tools. The frequency, timing, and debugging tools are discussed in Chapter 18.

The exporter reduces the problem of Ada program execution to the particular target program invocation conventions. As far as semantics are concerned, we can summarize by saying that the compiler, linker, importer and exporter only change the representation of an Ada program: they are binding transformations that leave the semantics invariant. (We have shown this in Figure 14.2.) In the next chapters, we examine the issues associated with incomplete programming, distributed programming, and debugging.

References
Ada runtime support tools are discussed in [4], [5], [6], [8]. APSE support for the target is addressed in [18] and [27]. The TASK is discussed in [27].

Problems
1. How can the optimizing options to a compiler influence the pragmatics associated with the execution of the compiled program?

2. How is the Ada implementation cycle of compile, link, export and execute different from the implementation cycle of other languages? Compare Ada to FORTRAN, Lisp, Basic and Pascal in this regard.

3. Discuss some possible problems (and solutions) associated with interfacing to another language which has parameter passing and procedure calling mechanisms that are different from Ada.

16

Incomplete
Programming

The LRM makes the following declaration in Section 10.2:

> *A subunit is used for the separate compilation of the proper body of a program unit declared within another compilation unit. This method of splitting a program permits hierarchical program development.*

We see how the Ada language supports hierarchical program development. This is seen in almost all texts on the Ada language. However, how does the APSE support hierarchical program development?

Let's now see how we can compile, link, export and execute separately compiled "incomplete" programs and then relink them together for our deliverable product.

An incomplete program consists of one or more Ada compilation units that do not make up a complete Ada program due to the following reasons:

(a) Even though the specifications of the library units have been compiled, there may be some missing bodies.

(b) Some subunit bodies (those bodies that were declared to be separate) are also missing.

Here's a simple example. Suppose the file L1_spec contains a package specification for package L1; file L2_all contains the package specification and package body for package L2, and file main_all contains the package body for procedure main:

```
package L1 is  --  in file L1_spec

    function Add(X:Integer)return Integer;

end L1;

--   Note that there is no package body supplied
--   in this file.
```

```
package L2 is  --  in file L2_all

    function Inc(X:Integer)return Integer;

end L2;

package body L2 is

    function Inc(X:Integer)return Integer

        is separate;

end L2;

--   Note that the body for the function Inc is not
--   in this file.
```

```
with L1; with L2;

procedure Main is  --  This is contained in file main_all.

begin              --  actions
```

Foo : = L1.Add(Z);

Bar : = L2.Inc(Z);

--

end Main;

We now want to compile and execute procedure Main as a main program even though the program is incomplete. This is desirable in hierarchical program development; we may wish to test the compilation units that have been written. We observe that if we compile and link all these files together (in the state that they are presently in) several exceptions may be raised when Main is executed.

One might think that this situation defeats the purpose of separate compilation because we cannot execute a program containing these separately compiled units without modifying the program. However, this is really not the case: we just have to be more careful. We now show two "tricks" that enable an A P S E user to execute his incomplete Ada program.

Our first trick involves linking procedure Main all by itself (after it was compiled). In this case, the A P S E linker may issue a warning since it did not find the all the files it was told to link with in the library (those files named in the WITH clauses of procedure Main). When Main executes, exceptions will be raised when Main calls Add or Inc. (As we observed above, these exceptions can be handled if Main is modified.) In this way, Main can be tested completely isolated from L1 and L2. This can all be accomplished by the following:

>compile main_all, my_lib

>link main, my_lib, main_lnk

>export main_lnk, my_lib, main_exe

-- Finally, execute on the target. If the target is the host:

>main_exe -- invokes the program

Suppose we now supply the body of package L1. We compile this body and create a new linked entity with

>link main,my_lib,main_lnk

that links Main with the specification and body of L1 and the specification and body of L2. The linker also produces a warning because it cannot find the body of Inc. When Main is again executed,
an exception is raised when Inc is called. Thus, Main and L1 can be
tested together. We can similarly test Main and L2 together (after
we supply the subunit for Inc), and we can (eventually) link everything together for a grand test.

This first trick is actually what is traditionally done in linking
large applications projects together. We have two problems with
this trick. First, exceptions raised when we execute Main can only
be handled if we modify our original Ada source text for Main. We
must remember to "unmodify" Main back. Second, there may be
subtle errors in our program that are masked by unhandled (or handled) exceptions. We may not know where to look if real errors
exist.

Trick number two is an APSE answer to these problems. We
simply use the stub tool:

>stub (compilation_unit = >L1,

library = > my_lib,

output = > 11_stub)

>stub (compilation_unit = >L2,

library = > my_lib,

output = >inc_stub,

unit_name = >Inc)

In our directory, two Ada text files are created. One is a
dummy (a "stub" or an "alias") for the package body L1, and one
is a stub for the subunit Inc. The contents of these files depend on
the APSE. In general, these files contain appropriately generated calls
to the TEXT_IO package (that puts the fact that the "stubbed"

units were called) with correct parameter references. What we do now is to compile the two stub files:

```
compile 11_stub,my_lib

compile inc_stub,my_lib
```

We then link Main with my_lib. When Main is executed, instead of having exceptions being raised, suitable messages will be output (to standard output) when Add and Inc are called. Main can then be tested. We next supply the real body of L1. We "recompile" and "relink" it. Main and L1 can now be tested. Similarly, Main and L2 can be tested, and eventually the entire system can be tested.

A traditional-minded person might say that he could have written those dummy package bodies and subprogram bodies with the editor tool. In fact, there is nothing in the APSE that prevents him from doing so. However, this may become tedious when these dummy bodies are several pages long. In addition, it is not in the spirit of Ada (or an APSE) for an Ada applications programmer to waste his valuable time on an otherwise repetitive activity of simple textual substitution.

The moral of this section is: Ada permits hierarchical program development and the APSE permits incomplete programming; incomplete programming is thus a natural extension of hierarchical development, provided that the right tools are available.

References
Stub generators are discussed in [4], [5], [6].

Problems
1. What exceptions can be raised when Main, L1, and L2 are (incompletely) compiled, linked, exported, and executed?

2. A procedure P is a main Ada program that utilizes the functions in packages A, B, C, and D. Show all the ways in which P, A, B, C, and D can be compiled, linked, exported, and executed.

3. Use the library tool to get a list of the names of the library files associated with all the incomplete programming examples in this chapter.

17

Distributed
Programming

We'll now examine runtime issues that are associated with Ada tasks. The RM states the following about task runtime semantics (in Chapter 9):

> *Tasks are entities whose executions proceed in parallel in the following sense. Each task can be considered to be executed by a logical processor of its own. . . . Parallel tasks (parallel logical processors) may be implemented on multicomputers, multiprocessors, or with interleaved execution on a single physical processor.*

The challenge of Ada tasking semantics is to come up with novel applications and implementations that can be denoted in Ada and supported by an APSE.

Ada allows tasks to be noncooperating or cooperating: they may talk to each other or they may not. Ada permits tasks to depend on (and therefore control) other tasks. Part of this task dependence is governed by the entry calling mechanism. The nature of this dependence may reflect different situations; here are a few examples.

If every task is its own master (or no task can control any other task) we have the "loosely coupled" situation called anarchy. No task waits for any other task.

If one task is designated the master and the rest slaves (that serve the master) then we have a situation commonly called a dictatorship. In this case, the dictator waits for his slaves to serve him, or the slaves take turns (and also wait) for the dictator to request service.

The other situation that we encounter is called a democracy. Periodically, the tasks select a master from among their ranks. Any task can be the master. The selection process can be conducted by vote.

These three task control situations are found throughout the Ada applications domain, from input-output servers in fault tolerant computer systems to "object-oriented" models of human interactions. Ada provides a convenient notation for these situations. However, Ada provides no hint for how these situations may be implemented in a real computer system.

Let's examine the A P S E support for the implementation and allocation of tasks on physical processors.

First, recall that a process is the physical realization of an Ada program; this realization also corresponds very closely to the continuation semantics of an Ada program as we observed in Section 1. Ada programs may be realized by one or more processes, and may also contain tasks; these tasks may be realized by one or more processes. A compiler implementation may specify that an Ada program is to be realized by several processes, where each process is given a certain "piece" of the Ada program. This can be useful in some situations involving parallel computations where some computations can be realized on separate processes. A human user may or may not have the power to help specify this process allocation within his program: such power is usually dependent on the capability of the target and the power of the compiler. This situation is found in most programming languages used for parallel or multiprocessing applications.

Ada provides the task construct to enable a flexible specification of parallel computation. A task may be realized by a single process or by several processes; again, this depends on the functionality of the Ada compiler and the target. In fact, an Ada main program can be considered a task (a task of the environment, as the RM reminds us in Chapter 9).

The basic method of Ada task communication is by the rendezvous. The rendezvous may be implemented by different process communication mechanisms on different targets: process communication is in general highly implementation dependent. One simple mechanism for process communication is the "message-passing" paradigm of SEND and RECEIVE primitives between processes.

In summary, tasks are realized by one or more processes. These processes execute and communicate on the target. In order to see how these processes execute on the target, we must first identify several different target configuration topologies.

The first topology specifies that all processes associated with an Ada program reside on a single target machine. This is really the traditional "time-sharing" model: process execution proceeds in an interleaved, "round-robin" fashion. Each process is allocated a certain amount of time in the target machine before the machine transfers control to another process. Thus, process allocation amounts to process scheduling. This topology is also typical of early Ada compiler implementations, especially when the target machine is also the host, and is very useful when task objects are created at runtime (as an access object) and must be allocated the machine resources as certain processes are spawned.

The second topology corresponds to the other extreme: one process per target and one target per process. This corresponds to the highest degree of distributed programming. In addition (to complicate matters further), the targets do not have to be identical machines: they can all be physically different.

The third topology offers the most flexibility: we allow an arbitrary number of targets to support an arbitrary number of processes. This will probably be the most popular topology for Ada applications (and the most difficult to implement). We would have to have a mechanism for specifying which processes are to be allocated to which targets. If several processes are allocated to a single target, then these processes then execute on that target in a time-shared fashion: we have then specified the first topology for this target. The processes that execute on their own target behave as in the second topology.

This topology encompasses the previous ones and would be the most natural for the applications. Already, in many Ada applications, we see pairs of tasks (where one would normally design only one). In these cases, one task is a scheduler of entry calls for the other "working" task. This actually helps avoid certain infinite waits ("livelocks" and "deadlocks") that result from an undisciplined use of the rendezvous.

What about the situation where a process may be split between two or more targets? We have stated that support for applications involving this multiprocessing situation may be highly dependent on the functionality of the target and the power of the compiler, and that this situation is seen in parallel processing "extensions" to other programming languages. This support may also be provided by particular Ada target implementations. However, such implementations may not be in the spirit of Ada since they do not encourage transportability. If we really want our single process to execute on two or more targets, our Ada applications programmer should have specified his multiprocessing intentions more precisely in terms of Ada tasks. Consequently, the process may not have to be split up into two targets in an implementation dependent manner; the Ada programmer could split them up on the Ada level to reduce the problem of target allocation to one of the three above topologies.

Now, let's examine some implementation problems for these topologies.

We know that all tasks of a given type "share" a common task body. If tasks are created at runtime (for example, as an access object), we do not know a priori how many tasks the program may spawn. This may lead to problems if we insist on having one task per machine and one machine per task. We may either not have enough tasks to go around (which is "inefficient") or, more likely, we may not have enough machines to go around.

One solution would be to allow only task bodies (not necessarily all task objects) to be implemented on a single process. One implication of this is that all tasks of a given task type must be implemented on the same target.

If tasks are only created at compile time (statically), and we do know a priori how many tasks the program will spawn, we may want to control how many tasks we want on each target.

Suppose we have a total of T targets and S task objects. A solution to our allocation problem is to allocate a number of task objects to a particular process, and then allocate each particular process to a particular target (since we know how many tasks they are and who they are). Thus, some tasks will be assigned to Target A, others to Target B, and so on.

There may be a problem (in efficiency) if not all processes are executing to their maximum extent on their targets. For example, three targets may be executing four processes, with Process(A) allocated to Target(1), and Process(B), Process(3) and Process(4) allocated to Target(3). Target(2) is thus not being used efficiently.

One solution is to provide the target system with a task scheduler (which may run on one of the targets). This scheduler makes sure that no targets are idle by asking what all the tasks and targets are doing and then allocating (during the application runtime) processes to targets (usually by means of some predefined algorithm).

We have surveyed some of the problems and issues surrounding runtime support for Ada tasks. We now show how the APSE can be used to build programs that may run on more than one target. These programs are called distributed programs.

Suppose procedure Main contains the specifications of two task objects, Dee and Dum. We want tasks Dee and Dum to execute (as two different processes) on two different targets. We also want Main to execute on a third target. How do we do it? Here is an APSE strategy that accomplishes this:

1. Make the task bodies of Dee and Dum subunits. Consequently, we have the following Ada text in the file my_main:

    ```
    procedure Main is

    --

      task Dee is

        ---

      end Dee;

      task Dum is

        ---

      end Dum;
    ```

```
-----

    task body Dee is separate;

    task body Dum is separate;

---

begin    --    actions for Main: start Dee and Dum

---

end Main;
```

The task bodies for Dee and Dum are in the files T_Dee and T_Dum:

```
separate(Main)

task body Dee is   --   in file T_Dee

---

end Dee;




separate(Main)

task body Dum is   --   in file T_Dum

--

end Dum;
```

We want to compile these three files into three libraries (reflecting the different targets):

```
main_lib

dee_lib

dum_lib
```

2. We are now ready for compilation. First:

   compile my_main,main_lib

   But what about the bodies of Dee and Dum that were specified in Main? We use an APSE trick.

3. Use the separator tool:

   separate(declaring_unit = >Main,

   declaring_library = >main_lib,

   task_name = > Dee,

   remote_library = > dee_lib)

   separate(Main,main_lib,Dum,dum_lib)

   What does this tool do? In main_lib, SEPARATE creates a dummy (an "alias") for the task bodies of Dee and Dum in the form of the library files main'dee'body and main'dum'body. Suitable references in these dummy task bodies will be generated for the linker. In dee_lib, SEPARATE creates a copy of the declaration part of Dee's declaring unit (the subprogram Main) in the form of the library file Main'dee'spec. SEPARATE also creates a copy of the declaration part for Dum in dum_lib in the form of Main'dum'spec.

4. Compile tasks Dee and Dum:

   compile T_Dee,dee_lib

   compile T_Dum, dum_lib

   Now dee_lib has the library file Main'dee'body and dum_lib has the library file Main'dum'body. Are we ready for linking? We first must specify the communication and control topology in a file that is used by the linker in one of the linker's parameters. What must the linker know?

187

(a) The linker must know who the "main program" is (the task that all other tasks depend on).

(b) The linker must be told who the dependent tasks are and how these tasks are controlled.

(c) The linker must be told which runtime support communication software must be loaded in order to support this topology. All this information must be created by the APSE user and placed in some file.

(d) The linker must know what other runtime support library packages are necessary for the execution of the program on the target.

5. Create the file my_top which contains topological information for the task control and communication between targets. The information containing the process allocation specification is specified to the linker in a similar way to that of a memory allocation specification (for an overlay).

6. Now link:

```
link(main_name => main,

    library => main_lib,

    output_name => linked_main,

    topology => my_top)


link(main_name => remote_task,

    library => dee_lib,

    output_name => linked_dee,

    topology => my_top)


link(main_name => remote_task,

    library => dum_lib,
```

output_name = > linked_dum,

topology = > my_top)

What does the linker do here? In addition to its normal functions, link consolidates the correct communication and control software for each target. All addresses and interrupts are specified. All this is now contained in the following three files in our directory:

linked_main

linked_dee

linked_dum

These three files will realize three processes on three separate targets.

7. We are now ready to export these files (in the conventional manner).

8. Once exported, this distributed program is ready to run. How is this program invoked?

If the targets (now physical processors) are now connected with the correct physical conections, when Main is invoked a message can be passed to initiate the processes corresponding to Dee and Dum. If the targets are incorrectly connected, some exceptions will be raised when Main is invoked.

We have some other problems regarding distributed programs. Because we use the separator tool, certain scope and visibility may be limited in the remote targets. In addition, certain machine dependencies may produce legitimate ambiguities. Different APSE tools may address these issues.

Thus, distributed programming is permitted in Ada but must be supported by special APSE tools, including a linker (with a topology option), a separator, and a collection of runtime support software to handle intertask control and communications.

References
Issues on implementing Ada on distributed targets are discussed in [39]. Style guidelines for writing distributed Ada programs are

found in [30]. Ada support for targets is discussed in [18] and [27]. The separator tool is described in [5].

Problems

1. Use the library tool to check which library files were created before, during, and after the use of the separator tool.

2. Take an Ada program that you wrote that contains Ada tasking constructs and show how this program may be distributed onto different targets. Explain your choice of topology.

3. What exceptions could be raised if the targets are incorrectly connected in a distributed program?

18

Debugging: Tools for Quality Assurance

We have finally produced an Ada applications program and have executed it. An important problem remains: How do we know if our compiled, linked, and exported Ada program will do what it is supposed to do? Are the original semantics of our Ada program correctly mapped to the semantics of the target machine execution? What APSE facilities are available to help us answer these questions?

We can answer these questions on several levels. They all come under the category of "quality assurance provisions." Software quality assurance is an activity that determines whether a developed system can be verified in regard to its fulfillment of requirements and its compliance to its technical design specifications. Quality assurance provisions in the form of some kind of formal verification and compliance plan will be required for certain collections of Ada programs. These special Ada programs (sometimes called Computer Program Configuration Items, or CPCI for short) are the ultimate deliverable product for our customer. They reflect the system requirements and are specified early in the design stage in the Ada life cycle. The several levels of quality assurance correspond to a series of tests:

1. Computer Programming Test and Evaluation (or CPT&E)
   This level of quality assurance testing provides for certain tests to be conducted before any "formal" test of quality. The tests included in this level are oriented toward the design and development stages of the Ada life cycle. Essentially, what is required here is the verification of the semantics of the implemented algorithms by the human who mapped the algorithm onto Ada program structures.

2. Preliminary Qualification Tests (or PQT)
   This level of testing includes a formal series of tests that attempt to verify the compliance of the Ada software components of a CPCI to its specifications. PQT usually occurs in the developer's APSE, and its goal is to verify the internal interfaces between the CPCIS and to check if all the CPCIS were implemented.

3. Formal Qualification Tests (or FQT)
   This level of testing includes a formal series of tests that are intended to verify the compliance of the integrated CPCI with its specifications. FQT usually occurs at the customer's site and in the operational environment. FQT is sometimes referred to as a System Level Development Test and Evaluation, since these tests integrate the CPCIS into an operational configuration that resembles the deliverable system as much as possible. One goal of the FQT is the verification of the external interfaces of the application with its environment.

There are other acronyms associated with quality assurance tests. Many of these test and evaluation procedures overlap. The exact name of these tests in a quality assurance plan in general depends on the customer. Other acronyms associated with quality assurance are concerned with a general review of the existing state of the application with a customer in order to ascertain progress, problems, solutions and changes. Here are some of these acronyms:

4. Development Test and Evaluation (DT&E)
   This level of quality assurance testing is concerned

with the evaluation of the lowest level of Ada software components. This evaluation primarily demonstrates the completion of the application life cycle design stage, shows that the implementation chosen has minimized any forseen risks, and presents a criteria that shows that the application satisfies its specification.

5. Initial Operational Test and Evaluation (IOT&E)

This level of testing is an attempt to determine an estimate of the effectiveness of the application in an operational environment. Part of the issues examined here would be those of interoperability and transportability, maintainability, and trainability.

6. Operational Test and Evaluation (OT&E)

This level of testing represents a more detailed evaluation of the usefulness of an application. This level investigates the issues of compatibility, reliability, logistics for support, cost of ownership and maintenance, personnel and management organizational requirements, and the introduction strategy. After the application is deployed, a Follow-On Operational Test and Evaluation (FOT&E) level may be necessary to evaluate changes made to the application, or simply to reevaluate the application with regard to newer operational requirements.

7. System Requirements Review (SRR)

This review is conducted to ascertain whether the requirements of an Ada application satisfies the functional requirements assocaited with what the customer wants, and how the Ada application will satisfy the customer's external and internal interface requirements.

8. Preliminary Design Review (PDR)

This review is conducted to ascertain whether the preliminary design of an Ada application corresponds to the Ada application specification, especially in regard to interface specifications.

9. System Design Review (SDR)

This review ascertains whether the Ada software components satisfy the general system requirements associated with configuration management, risk management, and test plans.

10. Critical Design Review (CDR)

> This review evaluates the detailed design of the Ada application, and determines whether the specification is sufficiently well understood so that an Ada programmer can complete the implementation.

11. Formal Qualification Review (FQR)

> This review evaluates the test reports and test data that is generated as part of a FQT. This review assures that all tests required by the quality assurance provisions of the development specification have been completed and that the Ada application performs as indicated by its requirements.

What are the differences between a formal and informal test plan? Formal test plans are documented procedures that have the approval of both the Ada applications developer and the customer; informal tests do not necessarily need the formal agreement of the customer. The degree of test "formality" is not an indication of the rigor of the test.

What activities are involved with quality assurance? The key activity is trying to find errors. These errors can be found by someone just looking at an Ada program. His experience and knowledge may tell him that a particular Ada construct will not work in a particular context, or that the Ada construct simply does not implement an algorithm that was previously specified. Errors can also be found by the analysis of repeated execution of tests. Depending on how well these tests are designed, it may take an extremely long time to find a single error. Finally, the real reason for finding errors in this quality assurance procedure is so they can be corrected and so that we can declare that the application works and does what it is supposed to do under its specified applications environment.

We have used several undefined terms in our examination of quality assurance. These terms are defined in several books on software engineering. Unfortunately, the definitions are not standard and frequently vary. The definitions that we have been using were culled from a variety of sources, the primary source being Reference [11]. Here are our definitions associated with Ada software quality assurance:

Test:

> A test is a procedure that is designed to obtain, verify, or provide data for the evaluation of the operational capability

of an Ada application or Ada software component. One way that this data can be obtained is by the execution of an Ada software component (or Ada application) with the intention of finding errors. These errors (or the lack of errors, or even particular Ada generated messages) can be used to evaluate the operation of the Ada software component.

Verification:

The Ada applications life cycle contains several stages, ranging from requirements to implementation. We may consider this cycle a "layer," similar to the ISO model that we have seen in Section 1. Consequently, these layers have the following interfaces: requirements-specification, specification-design, design-implementation, implementation-maintenance. Verification is the process of determining whether the interfaces between the various levels in this "Ada applications layered model" are consistent. Verification determines whether the specifications satisfy the requirements, whether the design satisfies the specification, whether the implementation satisfies the design, and whether the application can be maintained (which necessitates a "recursion" to the lower levels). Consequently, verification occurs in the requirements validation stage, in design reviews, in PQT and in FQT. In PQT, verification amounts to finding errors in the Ada program by evaluating it in the customer's environment.

Validation:

Validation corresponds to the cycle of evaluation, integration, and test activities that are performed on the system as a whole. Validation assures that the application system satisfies the requirements of the customer in the customer's operating environment. Validation also encompasses the prevention, detection, diagnosis and correction of errors.

Inspection:

A general review, appraisal, or test of any life cycle product (documentation, Ada text, executable units) that checks for conformity with standards or requirements.

Certification:

Certification confirms that a deployed Ada application system is verified and validated, is operationally effective, and satisfies its requirements under its specified operating conditions. A certified system formally guarantees its compli-

195

ance with its requirements (with a certificate). Certification requires an independent quality control board with its own set of acceptance tests. A validated Ada compiler is an example of a certified system.

Correctness assessment:

An Ada software component is evaluated to be correct, if it is demonstrated that its actual behavior is what was predicted. This demonstration may be in the form of a formal proof, an exhaustive series of tests, a simple series of tests, or an informal rationale.

Since the APSE is supposed to support the life cycle needs of an Ada application, there must be some APSE facilities to support the quality assurance of an Ada application. Much of this support relates to the planning and scheduling of tests, the evaluation of generated documentation, and the general project organization of the Ada application. Some of these facilities are supported by the APSE in the form of configuration management tools and resources. Other tools for quality assurance may be provided that aid the verification process; these tools may automate some of the testing and analysis tasks. The precise tools that are available for these tasks in general depend on the APSE.

What tools may be available on an APSE that support testing and analysis? Ideally, we would like a tool that would take an arbitrary Ada program as input and tells us whether it would work or not. This tool would also find and correct all errors that it knows about. If these answers were obtained without us having to execute our original Ada program, we would call such a tool a static analysis tool. If these answers were obtained after the execution of our program (at least once), we would call such a tool a dynamic analysis tool. There are some questions as to whether such a tool can ever be built. However, we can subset some of the capabilities of these types of tools.

Some of the static analysis tools that Stoneman mentions we have already seen in connection with the compiler. Tools like cross-reference listings can help us evaluate an Ada program without having it execute.

Powerful dynamic analysis tools are traditional in most existing programming support environments, and several are also mentioned by Stoneman. We have seen some of them in connection with the linker and exporter. These tools help us draw conclusions after (or during) the execution of our Ada program. They may tell us what the machine instructions of the Ada program are doing, and may also "unbind" these machine instructions into the original Ada text. How would these tools work? To enforce the "unbinding," we may have to provide special parameters to the compiler, linker, and exporter.

One useful tool in this regard is a timing analyzer. This tool can tell us how long our program (or how long a particular block of the program) takes when it runs.

A similar tool is the frequency analyzer. This tool can tell us what particular syntactical Ada constructs are being executed (if at all), and how many times such a construct is being executed.

The frequency analyzer and timing analyzer both provide information about the execution of an Ada program on the target. We note that in order to access this information, the target must have the capability of interacting with the user. This capability is supplied by the exporter.

One of the most traditional tools for dynamic analysis is the debugger. This is an interactive tool that helps a human analyze and correct errors in his Ada program. In the APSE, a user may be aided in his analysis with the following facilities provided by the debugger tool:

an executing Ada program may be interrupted and resumed;

data and control may be examined;

some variables may be modified;

the state of active subprograms, blocks, and tasks may be listed;

"breakpoints" may be inserted that provide a suspension when the program is symbolically executed;

a program may be symbolically executed "one step at a time."

The APSE user and all the tools interact on the host. The Ada program runs on the target. Consequently, the debugger is an APSE tool that is distributed between host and target. What is the nature of this distribution?

In general, the nature of this distribution depends on the APSE. One solution is to provide special communication and control software between the host and target (this time called "Debug Ada Support Kernal," or D A S K), with special information passed to the compiler, linker, and exporter. Of course this support is easier to implement if the target is the host: we do not have to worry about physical connections.

We now give a sample session with the DEBUG tool. We assume the host is the target.

>my_exe -- Run the program on the host (target).

1

2

3

4

5 -- An infinite loop?

ˆB -- We type control B to invoke the "breaker" tool.

B> -- Everything suspended. What can we do here?

B>?

EXIT

DESCRIBE

EXAMPLE

LOGOUT

SUSPEND

RESUME

START

STOP

DEBUG

B> Debug --Aha—help is on the way.

B>D>29: PUT(I+1); -- DEBUG shows us where we stopped

B>D>put i   -- my_exe.

    4   -- Put the value of an Ada variable.

B>D> list 26:30   -- List lines 26 through 30 in the program.

    26: GOTO <<HERE>>;

    27: <<HERE>> I:=I;

    28: I:=I+1;

    29: PUT (I+1);

    30: GOTO <<HERE>>;

-- (This is obviously a bad program.)

B>D> i:=0;   -- Let's see what happens with this assignment;

B>D> run 5   -- Execute the next 5 lines.

    30: GOTO <<HERE>>;

    27: <<HERE>> I:=I;

    28: I:=I+1;

    29: PUT (I+1);

      1

    30: GOTO <<HERE>>;

-- The error found by this user is that the variable *i* should
-- have been assigned to *j*. A "simple" syntax error.
-- Here is a simple correction:

B>D> set 27: <<here>> i:=j;

```
B>D>   list *  --   What are the values of all the variables?

        I = 0      J = 0       K = -9

B>D>   run  5

        27: <<HERE>> I: = J;

        28: I: = I + 1;

        29: PUT (I + 1);

            - 8

        30: GOTO <<HERE>>;

        27: <<HERE>> I: = J;

--   The user thought that he found all the errors!

B>D>exit   --   DEBUG tool

B> exit   --   the BREAK facility

>   --   Back to the CLP: what happenned to my_exe?
```

The target program denoted by my_exe was not modified in this interaction.

An APSE debugger can help an Ada programmer analyze the different syntactic structures in his program. Different APSES may provide different facilities for the analysis of tasks, the propagation of exceptions, the recursion of subprograms and the interrogation of complex data structures. An APSE debugger may also support the machine dependent features of Ada as well.

Debugger tools help eliminate some of the tedium associated with finding errors and diagnosing them. The nature of this tedious job has, perhaps, given us this unfortunate name for this aspect of quality assurance.

References
Quality assurance is discussed in [10], [11], [13], [14], [21], [33]. General criteria for the evaluation of an APSE is discussed in [19]

and [35]. APSE debugging requirements can be found in [17], [22] and [42]. Examples of APSE debuggers are in [4], [5], [6], [8].

Problems

1. Can testing find "all" errors contained in a program?

2. Construct an example where an exhaustive test of all control structures in an Ada program may take several hours, months, or even years.

3. Discuss the differences between a rigorous proof of program correctness, a series of convincing tests, and a three-sentence rationale that convinces a customer of the worthiness of the program. Which would you trust? Which is the most cost effective?

4. Discuss what features in an APSE debugger are desirable for (a) incomplete programming and (b) distributed programming.

SECTION FIVE
INTERFACE ISSUES

19

APSE
Interfaces

Let's review the Stoneman topology associated with an APSE. The APSE user is at the highest level. He has control and acccess over the next level: the MAPSE tools. These tools have control and access over the KAPSE. Finally, the KAPSE has control and access over the host machine computing resources traditionally established in the operating system of the host machine.

Recall that one of the virtues of this layered approach is the basic principle that if we standardize the interfaces to a particular level then the level immediately above this level is "permitted" to be interoperable and transportable. How this is accomplished is described in Section 1 as the Stoneman strategy for interoperability and transportability. The key assumption here is that this algorithm is feasible if there is a way to establish and validate standards for these interfaces.

Standardizing anything is somewhat tricky. We must make sure that we know why we are standardizing a particular interface and what (desired and undesired) consequences may result from this standardization. In addition, the question of validating a particular implementation's conformance to these standards is not trivial. If the standards are too strong they may be unsuccessful. If they are too weak they may also be unsuccessful.

In the APSE, we observe the following interfaces between levels:

APSE/User ⟷ MAPSE (Tools and Resources)
MAPSE ⟷ KAPSE
KAPSE ⟷ Host Operating System (Host Resources)

We also observe the following APSE interfaces for the target:

Ada Application Program ⟷ Target Ada Support Kernel
Target Ada Support Kernel ⟷ Target Operating System
(Target Resources)

The interfaces are denoted by bidirectional arrows. Processing entities are denoted to the left and to the right of these bidirectional arrows. We can consider this denotation as a classical data flow description: data (which can also in turn contain control information) flows between these processing entities. We can also make use of some standard techniques in the utilization of Ada as a program design language and describe the above denotation by a collection of Ada package specifications. In this case, the processing entities (the APSE-User, the MAPSE, the KAPSE, the Host Operating System, the Ada Application Program, the Target Ada Support Kernel, and the Target Operating System) may be described by Ada package specifications, with the interfaces being denoted by Ada functions, procedures, and entries defined within the package specifications.

We'll now examine the nature of these APSE interfaces with respect to the host.

The APSE/User-MAPSE interface is what the (human) user sees when he is talking to his APSE. Part of this interface is the command language for all interactive tools. This includes the command language for the MAPSE itself (the MCL), the command language for the editor, debugger, and so on. Another part of this interface is contained in the naming (binding) mechanism associated with pathnames. This interface is seen when the user is explicitly using the data base or special configuration management tools. This interface has a definite syntax and semantics that are usually different from the syntax and semantics associated with the Ada language. What would happen if we fixed the syntax and semantics of this interface to a particular standard? Fixing this interface essentially amounts to standardizing a set of MAPSE tools.

One of the facilities that the MAPSE-KAPSE interface provides is the essential tool communication mechanism. Stoneman declares that interoperability and transportability of Ada programs and tools can be accomplished at this level by following the strategy that requires the isolation of machine dependencies to the KAPSE. What happens when this interface is fixed? Standardizing this interface essentially standardizes the capabilities of a KAPSE.

The KAPSE-Host interface is where Stoneman specifies the "machine dependencies" to reside. Standardizing these interfaces effectively standardizes an APSE host operating system.

One interesting note at this point is that our current APSE experience demonstrates an interesting dualism between host and target. The interoperability and transportability characteristics that we observe on the host are also echoed on the target (and vice versa). This is especially true for the following host/target applications:

distributed programming
debugging
user interaction
input-output

The question boils down to properly identifying the desired runtime support that is rich enough to support Ada semantics.

Now, let's examine the APSE interfaces that are peculiar to targets.

The highest level interface that is observed at the target is the Ada Application Program-Target Ada Support Kernel interface. This interface is supplied when a human builds an Ada program that utilizes some service or resource that he knows is available to him on the target. For example, an Ada application program may have to open a file for input or output. Depending on the target facilities, a target may have its own mechanism for file naming, data base pathname association, or even configuration management. In fact, the target may even have a KAPSE residing on it! In this case, an Ada program that uses the Target Ada Support Kernel would in fact be using the KAPSE of another host. Fixing the interface to the Target Ada Support Kernel would aid in the transportability and interoperability of Ada applications.

The Target Ada Support Kernel-Target Operating System interface is supplied by what the TASK calls to the target operating system. This interface is responsible for supporting the Ada semantics on a particular target machine. One may say that it occupies the same place that the KAPSE occupies on the host: KAPSE utilization of the host operating system resources are similar to the TASK utilization of the target operating system resources. What if there is no target operating system? In this case, the interface is "virtual" and the target machine resources are totally provided by the TASK. Standardizing this interface would effectively standardize a target operating system. This would permit a high degree of interoperability and transportability (and therefore, retargetability) of Ada applications programs since all Ada applications would effectively reside on "one" target.

We conclude this section on interfaces by observing some benefits and risks associated with standardization.

The benefits to a standard set of APSE interfaces would be the increase of shared Ada programs. It is important to note that such a standardization does not, a priori, guarantee the availability of interoperable and transportable Ada software; it only makes the support for such software available.

One particular problem associated with standardization is the problem of either standardizing too much or too little. A "loose" standard may not produce the predicted benefits of the standard since there would be too much freedom of implementation choice (using this standard would be like using no standard). A "tight" standard may restrict the freedom of the implementors so that technological advances might be prohibited from being used (so the standard would have to be scrapped). We can illustrate some of these problems by examining the interfaces that might be standardized to assure the transportability of some interactive tools.

APSE tools that can be controlled by a human require an interface to support the interaction between a device that the human controls directly and the tool that is to be controlled. If we want these tools to be transportable across APSES, then KAPSE interfaces must be provided that support this interaction. These tools (and necessarily, their interfaces) are supported by special interactive hardware devices. MAPSE tools that are characterized by their important interactive features are command language processors, editors, and symbolic debuggers. Other APSE tools that have important interactive components are mail tools, configuration control tools, and display tools. To permit transportability, these tools communicate with the KAPSE and with a device interface that may model a terminal keyboard, a terminal display (CRT screen), a light-pen, or a "mouse."

Interactive tools interact with a human on a variety of levels. One basic taxonomy shows that these tools can be classified as having "menu," "fill-in-the-blanks," or "parametric" human interfaces. All MAPSE and APSE tools mentioned above can be classified by this taxonomy. Some tools and environments exploit this taxonomy by offering the human user a choice of various "modes." For example, a tool may initially assume a parametric mode but may then switch to a menu mode if the tool user is regarded as "inexperienced" by some time-out mechanism. These environments frequently use several images or "windows" displayed simultaneously on a screen (for output), and use pointing devices for input in addition to the terminal keyboard. We have seen an example of such a tool with our examination of the integrated editor in Section 3.

The Interlisp environment that Stoneman references (Section 4.D.4) is an example of one such environment. All tools are completely integrated since the command language of this environment is the same as the target application language. Some implementations support process invocation in conjunction with window creation, so that a human user can see how his tools invoked other tools. This gives the illusion of performing several tasks simultaneously at "different" terminals. When coupled with an input device used for pointing (frequently a mouse), human productivity is enhanced. Certain textual (keyboard) commands can be replaced by a menu mode, working in conjunction with pushbuttons on an input pointing device. This device can also be used to facilitate the movement of windows. This further gives the human more control over his interaction.

This multiple windowing capability is available not only in Interlisp. Several powerful editor tools support multiple windows on a variety of terminals. These tools are hosted on a variety of programming environments. Some tools exist that support a windowing capability and that are supposed to be transportable to several APSES.

In Section 4.D in Stoneman where several categories of interactive devices are specified, it is also observed that "the same control signals will be accepted by the terminal interface routines from all devices of these types." If these devices are to be supported in future APSES, and tools that use these devices are to be shared between APSES, standard interfaces must be provided to support "devices of these types." If these interfaces are not provided, transportability of tools that use these devices will be very difficult to achieve.

At this point, we observe that there may be a good deal of difficulty in transporting tools across APSES, even if we have rigorously defined KAPSE interfaces. The issue here is ultimately that of pragmatics in the form of hardware functionality. For example, a screen editor can hardly be transported to an implementation consisting of a teletypewriter. If it is assumed that "all" APSES to be built will only utilize teletypewriters, there may be a temptation to ignore the interface requirements for nonteletypewriter input-output devices. Even though this example is somewhat unrealistic, it shows that a danger exists with "tight" interface standards (reflecting present technology APSE tools and input-output devices). Consequently, the guiding philosophy should be to standardize interfaces that will not bias future tool builders. Otherwise, future tool builders would be forced to bypass these interfaces and build a tool that communicates directly with the host operating system, thus sacrificing the interoperability and transportability of such a tool.

References
An analysis of two different sets of APSE interfaces are presented in [23]. Issues associated with the TASK were first developed in [27]. A command language taxonomy is given in [38]. Tools that utilize windows are discussed in [31], [40], [47], [56]. Problems associated with APSE window tools are discussed in [9], [20], [25]. Pragmatic issues associated with Ada and APSEs are discussed in [55].

Problems
1. Discuss the different types of interfaces that may exist if there is no operating system on the host. How would this impact APSE users and tool writers? How would this impact interoperability and transportability?

2. Explain the difference between standardizing a KAPSE and standardizing the interfaces to the KAPSE.

3. Discuss the pros and cons of standardizing the interfaces to the APSE, MAPSE, KAPSE, and a host operating system.

20

Writing APSE Tools in Ada

The purpose of a KAPSE is to provide Ada programs with the special services that are "normally" supplied by an "operating system." What is the advantage of this intermediary? Instead of reimplementing all of our APSE tools for a different host, we "merely" reimplement the KAPSE for our particular host. Ideally, our tools do not have to be modified at all since all "host dependencies" are localized to the KAPSE. This rehostability effort represents possibly 20% of the effort required to rehost directly all the APSE tools.

As to how and when we can use this KAPSE, there are two situations:

1. Whenever we compile, link, and export a program whose intended target is the APSE host, the library support tools automatically bind the KAPSE with this program's runtime support libraries. Thus (at least on the host), the KAPSE consists of tools and resources that support a database, a toolset, and an interface. (This is why a KAPSE is called a

KAPSE: it really is a "kernel" APSE.) Similar runtime support also exists for the target in the TASK (but since our targets are usually embedded computer systems, this support is not as "powerful" as that for the host).

2. When an APSE user requests the KAPSE services directly in his program. After all, the KAPSE is implemented by a collection of Ada packages. These packages can be explicitly used in a program if they are referenced in a WITH clause.

What is exactly in those Ada packages for the KAPSE? Like all Ada packages, these KAPSE packages consist of two parts: package specifications (which serve as the interface to the KAPSE) and package bodies (which contain host dependent instructions.) These Ada packages are stored in a data base object. One implementation may have a directory called 'system(kapse). The APSE user then examines the Ada package specifications for the KAPSE in the object called 'system(kapse)'specification_listing.

How are these packages be used? Exactly like any other separately compiled Ada package. For example, here is part of the specification of one KAPSE package:

```
package KAPSE_TERMINAL_SUPPORT is

--   A package specification that contains the necessary
--   information for implementing Ada programs that
--   utilizes the KAPSE support for interactive video display
--   terminals. For example,

type TerminalType is limited private;

procedure Open (Terminal: in out TerminalType;

                Name: in String);

procedure Close (Terminal: in out TerminalType);

procedure EraseDisplay (Terminal in out TerminalType);

procedure Put (Terminal: in out TerminalType;

               Item:     in String);
```

```
procedure Get(Terminal: in out TerminalType;

                Item:     out String);

end KAPSE_TERMINAL_SUPPORT;
```

The implementation of this package provides the support for terminal input and output. The package specification serves as the interface to this support. It is not necessary to display the listing of the package body since it would undoubtedly be implemented differently for different machines. All that is necessary is a detailed description of what each Ada procedure or function does. The KAPSE interfaces are described in terms of Ada syntax (for the package specifications), semantics (that tells what the syntactic elements are for), and pragmatics (that may limit the use of certain entities because of some physical constraint).

One may wonder why we did not use the packages defined in Chapter 14 of the Ada RM. SEQUENTIAL_IO, DIRECT_IO, and TEXT_IO "define input-output operations applicable to files containing elements of a given type." The package LOW_LEVEL_IO "is provided for direct control of peripheral devices." None of these packages are applicable to the direct support of terminal interaction. The packages DIRECT_IO, SEQUENTIAL_IO, and TEXT_IO are too specific to files, and the package LOW_LEVEL_IO is too general (there is only a SEND_CONTROL and RECEIVE_CONTROL primitive that is available). Consequently, this support must be provided somewhere; we have seen that Stoneman requires this support be provided by the KAPSE.

To develop a transportable program that makes use of the interactive input output facilities available to us on our host, we must use the services provided by the KAPSE. (We can easily develop this program since we have the appropriate KAPSE packages available through the specifications). Our program can be developed just like any other separately compiled program:

```
with KAPSE_TERMINAL_SUPPORT;

procedure MyInteractiveProgram is

--  Some specifications and declarations, like
```

```
MyTerminal: KAPSE_TERMINAL_SUPPORT.TerminalType;

begin

--    Some actions that especially use the referenced KAPSE
--    package:

    KAPSE_TERMINAL_SUPPORT.Open (Myterminal, "George");

    KAPSE_TERMINAL_SUPPORT.get (MyTerminal, SomeString);


    KAPSE_TERMINAL_SUPPORT.EraseDisplay (MyTerminal);

end MyInteractiveProgram;
```

This Ada program is the contents of a data base object. We can compile this program into a program library that has our host as the intended target. Since our program is meant to run on our host, the KAPSE packages that are referenced are part of runtime support. The linker does all the rest. After we export the output of the linker into a data base object called My_Exe, this object can be executed. From the MCL we can simply invoke My_Exe with

```
> My_Exe
```

The effect of this invocation, among other things, would be in the appropriate terminal interaction.

At this point, you may ask, "Isn't the KAPSE supposed to be used in developing APSE tools?" The answer is that we *did* use the KAPSE in this way. Any Ada program that executes on the host (and in fact was developed on the host) can be an APSE tool if this program can be used by other Ada programs.

We have illustrated a simple use of KAPSE packages in the development of an Ada program that needs support for video display terminals. There are other KAPSE packages that provide support in other areas. Part of the effort of producing the Common APSE Interface Set (CAIS) is in specifying these areas of KAPSE support so that Ada programs can be transportable.

The CAIS is a set of standard KAPSE interfaces written in the form of Ada package specifications. KAPSE implementors who build their KAPSES that comply to these specifications help tool builders and program writers develop transportable and interoperable tools and programs. The CAIS support is divided into six areas:

1. The CAIS Node Model
    This section contains several Ada package specifications that provide the basis for the management of APSE entities such as files, directories, processes and devices.

2. CAIS Structure Nodes
    The specific support for the groupings of entities (directories, partitions, configurations) are provided by several Ada package specifications.

3. CAIS File Nodes
    The specific support for file objects are provided by several Ada package specifications. Part of this support is concerned with file input-output.

4. CAIS Process Nodes
    The specific support for processes are provided by several Ada package specifications. Part of this support is concerned with process control, process definition, process communication, process analysis, and process interrupts.

5. CAIS Device Nodes
    The specific support for teletypewriters, video display terminals, and other (interactive and noninteractive) devices are provided in several Ada package specifications.

6. CAIS Utilities
    This set off Ada package specifications provide for primitive services associated with text, list, and string manipulation.

The Ada package specifications for Version 1.3 of the CAIS are provided in the Appendix.

References
Specific issues relating to APSE terminal support are in [20]. The CAIS is described in [15] and [57].

Problems

1. Show how using a standard set of KAPSE interfaces like the CAIS can help a tool writer develop an interoperable and transportable tool.

2. Discuss the pros and cons of using a nonStoneman APSE, i.e., of developing an Ada program on a host that does not have a tool-set, data base, and interfaces that do not conform to the Stoneman requirements. What can you say about the ability of sharing resources on such an environment? of developing tools? of building portable applications programs? As an example, consider developing Ada programs on a host with the least Ada program support available (a LAPSE?): an Ada compiler, an Ada linker, an Ada library mechanism.

21

What makes
a KAPSE
a KAPSE?

KAPSE is a set of Ada packages. The specifications of these packages serve as the KAPSE interfaces. The bodies are the implementation of the KAPSE. Who uses the KAPSE? A human who desires to build tools or who desires to use the special services available to him if his target happens to be the host.

The semantics of the Ada package construct implies that a KAPSE user need only know the particular KAPSE specifications. He does not need to know (and indeed, one may want to prevent him from knowing) the details of KAPSE implementation. Standardizing these KAPSE interfaces makes life easier for the tool builder by permitting a high degree of tool interoperability and transportability.

What about the KAPSE bodies? Of course, they make a KAPSE a KAPSE. Different KAPSE bodies interface with different host operating systems, and, in general, these operating systems are not compatible.

We have seen in Section 1 that there are several good reasons to fix a set of standard KAPSE interfaces if one is to permit Ada program transportability and interoperability between different APSES.

This standard KAPSE interface is called the Common APSE Interface Set (CAIS). The CAIS makes life easier for tool builders and KAPSE users since the calls to all Ada KAPSE packages is the same. A KAPSE that complies to the CAIS provides KAPSE services to a KAPSE user with set syntax, semantics and pragmatics. Once tools are built using the CAIS, they can be easily rehosted. The standard "plug" (the Ada package specifications) fit all conforming KAPSEs.

Currently, the scope of the CAIS applies to Ada hosts only. CAIS support for the target is quite another matter. Part of the CAIS support for the target would involve standardizing the TASK interfaces. The issue of specifying the TASK is currently a very active area of investigation. Part of the problem here is in distributing the functionality between what a host is supposed to do and what a target is supposed to do. These issues are very dependent on computer technology that may or may not be available.

Specifying the standard KAPSE interface is difficult as it amounts to specifying an "Ada virtual machine." This "bottom-up" approach views the CAIS as a provider of the necessary host operating system primitives that cannot be provided directly. After a desired set of operating system resources are identified, a KAPSE that models these resources can be specified, and then its interfaces are standardized. Another way of looking at this problem is that we are defining the facilities that would be needed to build an APSE. This "top-down" view amounts to specifying the support that will be needed by APSE tools and resources. After a desired set of tools is identified, the KAPSE support for these tools can be specified and standardized.

Another aspect of a standard KAPSE interface is the necessity of providing a means of checking compliance to the standard. This can be seen in the context of KAPSE quality assurance. There are two levels of compliance to be demonstrated:

1. A KAPSE implementor's compliance (a CAIS implementation) to the CAIS Standard specification, and

2. CAIS specification compliance to CAIS requirements for program interoperability and transportability.

The first compliance activity can determine whether or not a KAPSE represents a verifiable and certifiable implementation. The second activity can determine whether or not the CAIS itself represents a verifiable and certifiable specification. Both activities can be regarded as part of an overall KAPSE verification activity. If the CAIS complies to its mission and operational requirements, and if a KAPSE complies to the CAIS specification, then the KAPSE complies to the CAIS mission and operational requirements.

What are the CAIS operational and mission requirements? Since the CAIS represents an (standard) interface to a KAPSE, part of the CAIS mission requirements are supplied by Stoneman. As we have seen in Section 1, Stoneman specifies a strategy that will permit interoperabiity and transportability of Ada programs: an Ada program can be moved from one APSE to another if the KAPSE interfaces that are referenced by the program are the same on both APSEs. The CAIS presents further technical and operational requirements that will permit program interoperability and transportability and also specifies certain pragmatic operational requirements that a KAPSE implementation must satisfy. Furthermore, the CAIS presents a formal specification of Ada packages that allocate the CAIS functional and operational requirements among identified functional areas.

A KAPSE can be regarded as a collection of Computer Program Configuration Items (CPCI) that implement the CAIS specification. KAPSE compliance to the CAIS is necessary to promote the Stoneman-recommended strategy for interoperability and transportability: Ada programs to be ported will have their machine dependencies isolated to the KAPSE interfaces. One method of determining KAPSE compliance to the CAIS is by developing a series of tests for the KAPSE as a system implementation of the CAIS specification. These tests can be designed to obtain and verify information for the evaluation of the operational capabilities of the KAPSE with regard to the operational capabilities of the CAIS specification. These tests can correspond to a standard sequence of formal and informal tests. Development Test and Evaluation (DT&E) and Computer Program Test and Evaluation (CPT&E) can be performed at the KAPSE implementor's site to verify the functionality of the KAPSE CPCI. A Preliminary Qualification Test (PQT) can also be performed at the KAPSE implementor's site to verify the capability of the KAPSE as a whole, for both tool writers and users, of other KAPSE resources.

Formal qualification tests can be developed for use by a certifying organization. This KAPSE system test will show if programs that use the KAPSE interfaces as specified by the CAIS will be ported to another APSE having a KAPSE that has already been certified. The Formal Qualification Test can incorporate a KAPSE verification matrix, cross-listing the KAPSE CPCI specification areas with the CAIS requirements.

The second compliance effort is concerned with determining whether the CAIS (as a specification) satisfies the operational, performance, and functional requirements associated with interoperability and transportability. This is necessary in order to follow the recommended Stoneman strategy for porting Ada programs between APSES. A key issue associated with this compliance effort is whether the CAIS can be used to specify a system that can be verified and certified. This issue is crucial if the CAIS is to be used for KAPSE certification. In addition, resolution of this issue can also help determine if the CAIS itself should be regarded as certifiable.

One method of determining whether the CAIS can be used to specify a verifiable system is by a series of design reviews. These reviews can be used to evaluate the completeness of the CAIS with respect to its requirements, as well as evaluating the particular functional capabilities of the CAIS with respect to its requirements. This evaluation can be facilitated by providing a formal notation for the functional capabilities of the CAIS packages. Another way that this evaluation can be facilitated is by building an operational prototype that implements the CAIS specification.

KAPSE compliance to a standard CAIS is necessary in order to permit the interoperability and transportability strategy recommended by Stoneman. The nature of this compliance is twofold. It is necessary to determine whether a KAPSE implementation complies with the standard CAIS so that a KAPSE can be certified. This compliance effort is available to all KAPSE implementors who desire to be certified. The second compliance criteria is concerned with CAIS compliance to CAIS requirements. This is necessary for the CAIS to be a certified specification.

We will now conclude with some brief observations regarding the use of Ada with and without a KAPSE.

The Ada language is a notation for specifying algorithms for embedded computer applications. As we observed in Sections 1 and 2, this notation is very useful at the specification and design stages for these applications. The APSE is meant to fully support the development of Ada applications throughout its lifecycle. Consequently, the APSE should provide automated aids to requirements, implementation, and maintenance stages of an Ada application. These automated aids are in turn supported by the KAPSE.

We have seen several examples of APSE tools that are used for Ada implementation and maintenance. The implementation tools are essentially the runtime support tools. They include compilers, linkers, exporters, importers and separators. The maintenance tools include those tools and facilities for configuration management. Tools that support the design and specification stages include listing tools, editors, and formatting tools. All of these tools depend in some manner on the KAPSE.

Let's briefly survey some current uses of Ada without a KAPSE.

Ada is frequently used as a notation to describe a system. This is an "incomplete" use of Ada, since we are only concerned in describing a system in Ada and (not necessarily) implementing it in Ada. Using Ada as a design notation is very powerful in building detailed system specifications. We note that using a computer programming language for this purpose is not new; ALGOL has been used this way for over 20 years, and Pascal has been used to specify several communications protocols. The use of Ada in this way as a Program Design Language and System Design Language has been described in several places. This utilization of Ada does not depend on an Ada compiler, an Ada linker, or an Ada library facility. There are no runtime facilities to support at all! The tools that may be used to support this use of Ada are formatting tools, and tools that help a human map his requirements into a design. Even though these facilities are provided by some APSE tools (supported by a KAPSE), there is no special need for KAPSE support. Any other toolset would be just as adequate. This is one example of using Ada without a KAPSE.

One "controversy" regarding the use of Ada as a design notation is whether to use a "subset" or "superset" of Ada. It should be made clear that these issues are not about the Ada language. The intentions of the RM are that the Ada language should not be subsetted or supersetted. The issues that the designers bring up are really about using Ada support tools to help this design process. This controversy is not about Ada; it is about the use of methodologies and support tools for the design.

References

The CAIS is described in [15]. References on quality assurance were detailed in Chapter 18. The use of Ada as a design notation is described in [26]. Other references on the use of Ada as a design language are in [45].

Problems

1. Show an example of two KAPSE packages whose specifications have the same syntax but whose bodies have different semantics.

2. Show an example of two KAPSE packages whose specifications have different syntaxes but whose bodies have the same semantics.

3. Show an example of two KAPSE packages whose specifications have the same syntax and whose bodies have the same semantics, even though the bodies have different syntaxes.

References

1. "Ada Programming Language Military Standard ANSI/MIL-STD-1815A," Ada Joint Program Office, January 1983.

2. "Formal Definition of the Ada Programming Language (Preliminary Version for Public Review)," Honeywell, Inc., Cii Honeywell Bull, INRIA, Ada Joint Program Office, November, 1980.

3. "Ada/Ed User's Guide," Version 1.1, New York University, Contract DAAB07-82-K-J196, CENTACS, April 1983.

4. "The Ada Study Team United Kingdom Ada Study, Final Technical Report," Department of Industry, London (England) 1981.

5. Ada Language System, A-5 and B-5 Specifications," Softech, Incorporated, Contract DAAK80-80-C-0507, CENTACS, February, 1982.

6. "Ada Integrated Environment, A-5 and B-5 Specifications," Intermetraics, Incorporated, Contract F30602-80-C-0291, RADC, November, 1982.

7. "Karlsruhe Ada Environment User Manual ENV-01," Ada Implementation Group, University of Karlsruhe, July, 1983.

8. "Ada Development Environment Reference Manual," 493-15011-01 (Revision 2), Rolm Corporation, October, 1983.

9. "APSE Interactive Monitor Draft Preliminary Program Specification," Texas Instruments, Incorporated, Contract N6601-82-C-0440, NOSC, February, 1983.

10. "Configuration Management System Interim Report on Interface Analysis," Computer Sciences Corporation, Contract N00123-80-D-0364, NOSC, August, 1982.

11. "Configuration Management Definitions for Digital Computer Programs," Configuration Management Bulletin No. 4-1, Electronic Industries Association G-33 Committee, May, 1982.

12. "Data Processing—Open Systems Interconnection, Basic Reference Model," International Standards Organization Draft International Standard 7498, 1978.

13. "Configuration Management Practices for Systems, Equipment, Munitions, and Computer Programs," "MIL-STD-483 (USAF), Air Force Systems Command, March 1979.

14. "Weapon System Software Development," MIL-STD-1679 (NAVY), NAVMAT, December, 1978.

15. "Draft Specification of the Common APSE Interface Set (CAIS)," Version 1.1, KIT/KITIA CAIS Working Group, Ada Joint Program Office, October, 1983. Also described in the "KIT/KITIA CAIS CAISWG Public Review of the Draft Specifications of the Common APSE Interface Set," (B. Schaar, Moderator), Ada Joint Program Office, September 14-15, 1983.

16. Beckman, F., *Mathematical Foundations of Programming*, Addison-Wesley, Reading, 1980.

17. Buxton, J., " "Stoneman" Requirements for Ada Programming Support Environments," NTIS ADA-100404, February, 1980.

18. Beane, J., "APSE Support for Targets," in [43].

19. Castor, V., "Critera for the Evaluation of Rolm Corporation's Ada Work Center," AFWAL/AAAF Wright-Patterson Air Force Base, January, 1983.

20. Cox, F., "KAPSE Support for Program/Terminal Interaction," in [44].

21. Durachka, R., "Software Engneering Standards and Practices," NASA Report 82148, June, 1981.

22. Fairley, R., "Ada Debugging and Testing Support Environments," in ACM SIGPLAN Notices, Volume 15, Number 11, November, 1980, pp. 16-25.

23. Foidl, J., "Interface Analysis of the Ada Integrated Environment and the Ada Language System," in [43].

24. Freedman, R., "Specifying KAPSE Interface Semantics," in [43].

25. Freedman, R., "Of Mice and Command Languages: KAPSE Support for Interactive Tools," in [44].

26. Freedman, R., *Programming Concepts with the Ada Language*, Petrocelli Books, Inc., Princeton, 1982.

27. Gargaro, A., Program Invocation and Control," in [43].

28. Goodenough, J., "Ada Compiler Validation Implementer's Guide," NTIS ADA-091760, October, 1980.

29. Goos, G., Wulf, W. (editors), "Diana Reference Manual," Karlsruhe University and Carnegie-Mellon University, March, 1981.

30 Hibbard, P., Hisgen, A., Rosenberg, J., Sherman, M., "Programming in Ada: Examples," Carnegie-Mellon University Report CMU-CS-80-149, October, 1980. Reprinted in: *Studies in Ada Style*, Springer-Verlag, New York, 1981.

31. Hopgood, F., "GKS (Graphical Kernel System): The First Graphics Standard," Science and Engineering Research Council, Chilton (England), January, 1982.

32. Houghton, R., "A Taxonomy of Tool Features for the Ada Programming Support Environment (APSE)," National Bureau of Standards (Draft), August, 1982.

33. Jensen, W., Tonies, C. (editors), *Software Engineering*, Prentice-Hall, Engelwood Cliffs, 1979. Also see: Shooman, M., *Software Engineering*, McGraw-Hill Book Co., New York, 1983.

34. Johnson, R., "KAPSE Model of VMS System Services," in [43].

35. Kafura, D., Lee, J., Lindquist, T., Probert, T., "Validation in Ada Programming Support Environments," in [43].

36. Kini, V., Martin, D., Stoughton, A., "Testing the INRIA Ada Formal Definition: The USC-ISI Formal Semantics Project," Proceedings of the AdaTEC Conference on Ada, ACM 825821, October, 1982, pp. 120-128.

37. Langsford, A., "Open Systems Interconnection—An Architecture for Interconnection or for Distributed Processing?," *Journal of Telecommunication Networks*, Volume 1, Number 3, Fall 1982, pp. 253-263.

38. Lindquist, T., "A Taxonomy of Command Language Features and Needed Underlying Support," Department of Computer Science Technical Report, Virginia Polytechnic Institute, November, 1983.

39. McDermid, J., "Ada on Multiple Processors," Royal Signals and Radar Establishment Memorandum 3464, Controller HMSO, London (England) March 1982.

40. Meyrowitz, N., van Dam, A., "Interactive Editing Systems (Part I and II)," ACM Computing Surveys, Volume 14, Number 3, September 1983, pp. 321-415.

41. Mooers, C., "The Hermes Guide," Bolt Beranek and Newman, Inc., Report 4995, August, 1982.

42. Mullerburg, M., "The Role of Debugging within Software Engineering Environments," *ACM Software Engineering Notes*, Volume 8, Number 4, August 1983, pp. 81-90.

43. Oberndorf, P., "Kernel Ada Programming Support Environment (KAPSE) Interface Team: Public Report Volume II," NOSC Technical Document 552, October, 1982.

44. Oberndorf, P., "Kernel Ada Programming Support Environment (KAPSE) Interface Team: Public Report Volume III," NOSC Technical Document October, 1983.

45. Romanowsy, H., "Ada Publications," *ACM Ada Letters*, Volume II, Number 6, May 1983, pp. 87-109.

46. Ryer, M., "Software Environments: The Unix Lessons," Intermetrics, Incorporated, 1982. Parts reprinted in: "Developing an Ada Programming Support Environment," *Mini-Micro Systems*, Volume 15, Number 9, September, 1982, pp. 223-226.

47. Stallman, R., "EMACS Manual for TWENEX Users," AI Memo 556, Artificial Intelligence Laboratory, MIT, Cambridge, August, 1980.

48. Standish, T., "New Category—Extensibility," in [43].

49. Stoy, J., "Denotational Semantics: The Scott-Strachey Approach to Programming Language Theory," MIT Press, Cambridge, May, 1979.

50. Teitelman, W., "Interlisp Reference Manual," Bolt Beranek and Newman and Xerox Corporation, October, 1978.

51. Tennent, R., *Principles of Programing Languages*, Prentice-Hall International, Engelwood Cliffs, 1981.

52. Turing, A., "On Computable Numbers with an Application to the Entscheidungsproblem," Proceedings of the London Mathematical Society, Volume 42 (Ser. 2), 1936, pp. 230-265.

53. Wand, M., "Deriving Target Code as a Representation of Continuation Semantics," ACM Transactions on Programming Languages and Systems, volume 14, Number 3, July, 1982, pp. 496-517.

54. Whitehill, S., "An Ada Virtual Operating System," Proceedings of the AdaTEC Conference on Ada, ACM 825821, October, 1982, pp. 238-250.

55. Willman, H., "Ada/APSE Portability: A Recommendation for Pragmatic Limitations," in [43].

56. Wirth, N., *Programming in Modula-2*, Springer-Verlag, New York, 1982.

57. *Proposed Military Standard Common APSE Interface Set (CAIS) Version 1.3*, KIT/KITIA CAIS Working Group, Fall 1984.

Appendix
CAIS Version 1.3
Package
Specifications

T his appendix contains a set of Ada package specifications of the CAIS (as defined in [57]) which compiles correctly.
Users of specific interfaces would have to instantiate the particular
generic packages. This arrangement of the package specifications
emphasizes encapsulation. The CAIS package bodies may or may
not be implemented entirely in Ada.

```
with text_io,
     io_exceptions;
package CAIS is

    type CAIS_FILE_TYPE is limited private;

    type TEXT_TYPE      is limited private;
    type NODE_TYPE      is limited private;
    type TERMINAL_TYPE is limited private;
    type NODE_KIND is (FILE, STRUCTURAL, PROCESS, DEVICE);
    type INTENT_SPECIFICATION is
        (EXISTENCE, READ, WRITE, READ_ATTRIBUTES, WRITE_ATTRIBUTES,
         APPEND_ATTRIBUTES, READ_RELATIONSHIPS, WRITE_RELATIONSHIPS,
```

APPEND_RELATIONSHIPS, READ_CONTENT, WRITE_CONTENT,
APPEND_CONTENT, CONTROL, EXECUTE, EXCLUSIVE_READ,
EXCLUSIVE_WRITE, EXCLUSIVE_READ_ATTRIBUTES,
EXCLUSIVE_WRITE_ATTRIBUTES, EXCLUSIVE_APPEND_ATTRIBUTES,
EXCLUSIVE_READ_RELATIONSHIPS, EXCLUSIVE_WRITE_RELATIONSHIPS,
EXCLUSIVE_APPEND_RELATIONSHIPS, EXCLUSIVE_READ_CONTENT,
EXCLUSIVE_WRITE_CONTENT, EXCLUSIVE_APPEND_CONTENT,
EXCLUSIVE_CONTROL);

```
type INTENTION is array (POSITIVE range <>) of INTENT_SPECIFICATION;
type PROCESS_STATUS is (READY, SUSPENDED, ABORTED, TERMINATED);
type COMPLETION_STATUS is (NOT_COMPLETED, ABORTED, TERMINATED);
type TERMINAL_CLASS is (SCROLL, PAGE, FORM);
type ACTIVE_POSITION is
    record
        LINE     : POSITIVE;
        COLUMN : POSITIVE;
    end record;

subtype LIST_TYPE is TEXT_TYPE;

subtype NAME_STRING      is STRING;
subtype FORM_STRING      is STRING;
subtype RELATIONSHIP_KEY is STRING;
subtype RELATION_NAME    is STRING;
subtype ATTRIBUTE_NAME   is STRING;


TOP_LEVEL        : constant NAME_STRING      := "'CURRENT_USER";
CURRENT NODE     : constant NAME_STRING      := "'CURRENT_NODE";
CURRENT_PROCESS  : constant NAME_STRING      := ".";
LATEST_KEY       : constant RELATIONSHIP_KEY := "#";
ROOT_PROCESS     : constant NAME_STRING      := "'CURRENT_JOB";
DOT              : constant RELATION_NAME    := "DOT";


function CURRENT_INPUT    return NAME_STRING;
function CURRENT_OUTPUT   return NAME_STRING;


STATUS_ERROR       : exception;
NAME_ERROR         : exception;
USE_ERROR          : exception;
LAYOUT_ERROR       : exception;
LOCK_ERROR         : exception;
ACCESS_VIOLATION   : exception;
SECURITY_VIOLATION : exception;


generic
    type INDEX is range <>;
package TEXT_UTILS is
```

230

```
function LENGTH (TEXT : TEXT_TYPE)    return INDEX;
function VALUE   (TEXT : in TEXT_TYPE) return STRING;
function EMPTY   (TEXT : in TEXT_TYPE) return BOOLEAN;

procedure INIT_TEXT (TEXT : in out TEXT_TYPE);
procedure FREE_TEXT (TEXT : in out TEXT_TYPE);

function TO_TEXT (STR   : in STRING)       return TEXT_TYPE;
function TO_TEXT (CHAR : in CHARACTER) return TEXT_TYPE;

function "&" (LEFT    : in TEXT_TYPE;
              RIGHT : in TEXT_TYPE)   return TEXT_TYPE;
function "&" (LEFT    : in TEXT_TYPE;
              RIGHT : in STRING)       return TEXT_TYPE;
function "&" (LEFT    : in STRING;
              RIGHT : in TEXT_TYPE)   return TEXT_TYPE;
function "&" (LEFT    : in TEXT_TYPE;
              RIGHT : in CHARACTER) return TEXT_TYPE;
function "&" (LEFT    : in CHARACTER;
              RIGHT : in TEXT_TYPE)   return TEXT_TYPE;

function "="  (LEFT    : in TEXT_TYPE;
               RIGHT : in TEXT_TYPE) return BOOLEAN;
function "<=" (LEFT    : in TEXT_TYPE;
               RIGHT : in TEXT_TYPE) return BOOLEAN;
function "<"  (LEFT    : in TEXT_TYPE;
               RIGHT : in TEXT_TYPE) return BOOLEAN;
function ">=" (LEFT    : in TEXT_TYPE;
               RIGHT : in TEXT_TYPE) return BOOLEAN;
function ">"  (LEFT    : in TEXT_TYPE;
               RIGHT : in TEXT_TYPE) return BOOLEAN;

procedure SET (OBJECT : in out TEXT_TYPE;
               VALUE  : in     TEXT_TYPE);
procedure SET (OBJECT : in out TEXT_TYPE;
               VALUE  : in     STRING);
procedure SET (OBJECT : in out TEXT_TYPE;
               VALUE  : in     CHARACTER);

procedure APPEND (TAIL : in     TEXT_TYPE;
                  TO   : in out TEXT_TYPE);
procedure APPEND (TAIL : in     STRING;
                  TO   : in out TEXT_TYPE);
procedure APPEND (TAIL : in     CHARACTER;
                  TO   : in out TEXT_TYPE);

procedure AMEND (OBJECT   : in out TEXT_TYPE;
                 BY       : in TEXT_TYPE;
                 POSITION : in INDEX);
```

231

```
      procedure AMEND (OBJECT   : in out TEXT_TYPE;
                       BY        : in STRING;
                       POSITION : in INDEX);
      procedure AMEND (OBJECT   : in out TEXT_TYPE;
                       BY        : in CHARACTER;
                       POSITION : in INDEX);

      function LOCATE (FRAGMENT : in TEXT_TYPE;
                       WITHIN    : in TEXT_TYPE)  return INDEX;
      function LOCATE (FRAGMENT : in STRING;
                       WITHIN    : in TEXT_TYPE)  return INDEX;
      function LOCATE (FRAGMENT : in CHARACTER;
                       WITHIN    : in TEXT_TYPE)  return INDEX;

end TEXT_UTILS;



generic
    type COUNT is range <>;
package LIST_UTILS is
    subtype  POSITIVE_COUNT is COUNT range 1 .. COUNT'LAST;
    subtype  LIST_TYPE      is TEXT_TYPE;
    subtype  KEY_STRING     is STRING;
    type ITEM_KIND is (LIST, IDENTIFIER, NUMBER, QUOTED_STRING);

    procedure INIT_LIST (LIST : in out LIST_TYPE);
    procedure FREE_LIST (LIST : in out LIST_TYPE);

    function IS_EMPTY        (LIST : in LIST_TYPE) return BOOLEAN;
    function KIND            (LIST : in LIST_TYPE) return ITEM_KIND;
    function QUOTED_STRING (LIST : in LIST_TYPE) return STRING;
    function IDENTIFIER      (LIST : in LIST_TYPE) return STRING;
    function NUMBER          (LIST : in LIST_TYPE) return INTEGER;

    procedure TO_LIST_QUOTED (LIST  : in out LIST_TYPE;
                              FROM : in    STRING);
    procedure TO_LIST        (LIST  : in out LIST_TYPE;
                              FROM : in    STRING);
    procedure TO_LIST        (LIST  : in out LIST_TYPE;
                              FROM : in    INTEGER);

    procedure SET (LIST  : in out LIST_TYPE;
                   VALUE : in    LIST_TYPE);

    function NUM_POSITIONAL  (LIST : in    LIST_TYPE) return COUNT;
    procedure ADD_POSITIONAL (LIST : in out LIST_TYPE;
                              ITEM : in    LIST_TYPE);
```

```
procedure ADD_POSITIONAL  (LIST  : in out LIST_TYPE;
                           ITEM : in     CHARACTER);


procedure GET_POSITIONAL (LIST       : in     LIST_TYPE;
                          ITEM       : in out LIST_TYPE;
                          POSITION : in     POSITIVE_COUNT);
procedure SET_POSITIONAL  (LIST          : in out LIST_TYPE;
                           ITEM       : in     LIST_TYPE;
                           POSITION : in     POSITIVE_COUNT);


function NUM_NAMED (LIST : in LIST_TYPE) return COUNT;


procedure ADD_NAMED (LIST        : in out LIST_TYPE;
                     KEYWORD : in     KEY_STRING;
                     ITEM        : in     LIST_TYPE);
procedure ADD_NAMED (LIST        : in out LIST_TYPE;
                     KEYWORD : in     KEY_STRING;
                     ITEM        : in     CHARACTER);


procedure GET_NAMED  (LIST        : in     LIST_TYPE;
                      ITEM        : in out LIST_TYPE;
                      POSITION : in     KEY_STRING);
procedure GET_NAMED  (LIST        : in     LIST_TYPE;
                      ITEM        : in out LIST_TYPE;
                      POSITION : in     POSITIVE_COUNT);


procedure SET_NAMED   (LIST        : in out LIST_TYPE;
                       ITEM        : in     LIST_TYPE;
                       POSITION : in     KEY_STRING);
procedure SET_NAMED   (LIST        : in out LIST_TYPE;
                       ITEM        : in     LIST_TYPE;
                       POSITION : in     POSITIVE_COUNT);


function KEYWORD (LIST         : in LIST_TYPE;
                  POSITION : in POSITIVE_COUNT) return Key_STRING;

end LIST_UTILS;


generic
package NODE_MANAGEMENT is

procedure OPEN (NODE          : in     NODE_TYPE;
                NAME          : in     NAME_STRING;
                INTENT        : in     INTENTION;
                TIME_LIMIT : in     DURATION := DURATION'FIRST);

procedure OPEN (NODE          : in out NODE_TYPE;
                BASE          : in     NODE_TYPE;
```

```
                    KEY        : in    REALATIONSHIP_KEY;
                    RELATION   : in    RELATION_NAME := DOT;
                    INTENT     : in    INTENTION;
                    TIME_LIMIT : in    DURATION := DURATION'FIRST);

procedure CLOSE (NODE : in out NODE_TYPE);
function IS_OPEN (NODE : in     NODE_TYPE) return BOOLEAN;
function KIND    (NODE : in     NODE_TYPE) return NODE_KIND;

procedure CHANGE_INTENT (NODE        : in out NODE_TYPE;
                         INTENT     : in    INTENTION;
                         TIME_LIMIT : in    DURATION
                                             := DURATION'FIRST);

function PRIMARY_NAME (NODE : in NODE_TYPE) return NAME_STRING;
function PRIMARY_KEY     (NODE : in NODE_TYPE return RELATIONSHIP_KEY;
function PRIMARY_RELATION (NODE : in NODE_TYPE) return RELATION_NAME;

function PATH_KEY       (NODE : in NODE_TYPE) return RELATIONSHIP_KEY;
function PATH_RELATION (NODE : in NODE_TYPE) return RELATION_NAME;

function OBTAINABLE (NODE    : in NODE_TYPE)           return BOOLEAN;
function OBTAINABLE (NAME    : in NAME_STRING)         return BOOLEAN;
function OBTAINABLE (BASE    : in NODE_TYPE;
                     KEY     : in RELATIONSHIP_KEY;
                     RELATION : in RELATION_NAME)      return BOOLEAN;

procedure GET_PARENT (NODE   : in    NODE_TYPE;
                      PARENT : in out NODE_TYPE);

procedure COPY_NODE (FROM : in NODE_TYPE;
                     TO   : in NAME_STRING);
procedure COPY_NODE (FROM        : in NODE_TYPE;
                     TO_BASE     : in NODE_TYPE;
                     TO_KEY      : in RELATIONSHIP_KEY;
                     TO_RELATION : in RELATION_NAME := DOT);

procedure COPY_TREE (FROM : in NODE_TYPE;
                     TO   : in NAME_STRING);
procedure COPY_TREE (FROM        : in NODE_TYPE;
                     TO_BASE     : in NODE_TYPE;
                     TO_KEY      : in RELATIONSHIP_KEY;
                     TO_RELATION : in RELATION_NAME := DOT);

procedure RENAME (NODE        : in NODE_TYPE;
                  NEW_NAME    : in NAME_STRING);
procedure RENAME (NODE        : in NODE_TYPE;
                  NEW_BASE    : in NODE_TYPE;
```

```
                         NEW_KEY         : in RELATIONSHIP_KEY;
                         NEW_RELATION : in RELATION_NAME := DOT);

procedure LINK (OLD_NAME       : in NAME_STRING;
               NEW_PATH        : in NAME_STRING);
procedure LINK (NODE           : in NODE_TYPE;
               NEW_BASE        : in NODE_TYPE;
               NEW_KEY         : in RELATIONSHIP_KEY;
               NEW_RELATION : in RELATION_NAME := DOT);


procedure UNLINK (NAME         : in NAME_STRING);
procedure UNLINK (BASE         : in NODE_TYPE;
                 KEY           : in RELATIONSHIP_KEY;
                 RELATION      : in RELATION_NAME := DOT);


procedure DELETE_NODE (NAME : in    NAME_STRING);
procedure DELETE_NODE(NODE : in out NODE_TYPE);
procedure DELETE_TREE  (NAME : in    NAME_STRING);
procedure DELETE_TREE  (NODE : in out NODE_TYPE);


type    NODE_ITERATOR                is private;
subtype RELATIONSHIP_KEY_PATTERN is RELATIONSHIP_KEY;
subtype RELATION_NAME_PATTERN    is RELATION_NAME;


procedure ITERATE   (ITERATOR       : in out NODE_ITERATOR;
                     NODE           : in     NODE_TYPE;
                     KIND           : in     NODE_KIND;
                     KEY            : in RELATIONSHIP_KEY_PATTERN := "*";
                     RELATION       : in RELATION_NAME_PATTERN := DOT;
                     PRIMARY_ONLY :in     BOOLEAN := TRUE);


procedure ITERATE   (ITERATOR       : in out NODE_ITERATOR;
                     NAME           : in     NAME_STRING;
                     KIND           : in     NODE_KIND;
                     KEY            : in RELATIONSHIP_KEY_PATTERN := "*";
                     RELATION       : in RELATION_NAME_PATTERN := DOT;
                     PRIMARY_ONLY : in     BOOLEAN := TRUE);


function MORE (ITERATOR : in NODE_ITERATOR) return BOOLEAN;


procedure GET_NEXT (ITERATOR      : in out NODE_ITERATOR;
                   NEXT_NODE : in out NODE_TYPE);


procedure SET_CURRENT_NODE (NAME : NAME_STRING);
procedure SET_CURRENT_NODE (NODE : NAME_STRING);


procedure GET_CURRENT_NODE (NODE : in out NODE_TYPE);
```

```
    function IS_SAME (NAME1 : in NAME_STRING;
                      NAME2 : in NAME_STRING) return BOOLEAN;

    function IS_SAME (NODE1 : in NODE_TYPE;
                      NODE2 : in NODE_TYPE) return BOOLEAN;

private
    type NODE_ITERATOR is (IMPLEMENTOR_WILL_DEFINE);
end NODE_MANAGEMENT;

generic
package ATTRIBUTES is

    type    ATTRIBUTE_ITERATOR is private;
    subtype ATTRIBUTE_PATTERN  is STRING;

    procedure CREATE_NODE_ATTRIBUTE (NAME   : in NAME_STRING;
                                     ATTRIB : in ATTRIBUTE_NAME;
                                     VALUE  : LIST_TYPE);
    procedure CREATE_NODE_ATTRIBUTE (NODE   : in NODE_TYPE;
                                     ATTRIB : in ATTRIBUTE_NAME;
                                     VALUE  : in LIST_TYPE);

    procedure CREATE_PATH_ATTRIBUTE  (NAME     : in NAME_STRING;
                                      ATTRIB   : in ATTRIBUTE_NAME;
                                      VALUE    : in LIST_TYPE);
    procedure CREATE_PATH_ATTRIBUTE  (BASE     : in NODE_TYPE;
                                      KEY      : in RELATIONSHIP_KEY;
                                      RELATION : in RELATION_NAME : = DOT;
                                      ATTRIB   : in ATTRIBUTE_NAME;
                                      VALUE    : in LIST_TYPE;

    procedure DELETE_NODE_ATTRIBUTE (NAME   : in NAME_STRING;
                                     ATTRIB : in ATTRIBUTE_NAME);
    procedure DELETE_NODE_ATTRIBUTE (NODE   : in NODE_TYPE;
                                     ATTRIB : in ATTRIBUTE_NAME);

    procedure DELETE_PATH_ATTRIBUTE (NAME     : in NAME_STRING;
                                     ATTRIB   : in ATTRIBUTE_NAME);
    procedure DELETE_PATH_ATTRIBUTE (BASE     : in NODE_TYPE;
                                     KEY      : in RELATIONSHIP_KEY;
                                     RELATION : in RELATION_NAME : = DOT;
                                     ATTRIB   : in ATTRIBUTE_NAME);

    procedure SET_NODE_ATTRIBUTE (NAME   : in NAME_STRING;
                                  ATTRIB : in ATTRIBUTE_NAME;
                                  VALUE  : in LIST_TYPE);
```

```
procedure SET_NODE_ATTRIBUTE (NODE    : in NODE_TYPE;
                              ATTRIB : in ATTRIBUTE_NAME;
                              VALUE : in LIST_TYPE);
procedure SET_PATH_ATTRIBUTE (NAME     : in NAME_STRING;
                             ATTRIB    : in ATTRIBUTE_NAME;
                             VALUE     : in LIST_TYPE);
procedure SET_PATH_ATTRIBUTE  (BASE     : in NODE_TYPE;
                              KEY       : in RELATIONSHIP_KEY;
                              RELATION : in RELATION_NAME : = DOT;
                              ATTRIB    : in ATTRIBUTE_NAME;
                              VALUE    : in LIST_TYPE);
procedure GET_NODE_ATTRIBUTE (Name   : in    NAME_STRING;
                              ATTRIB : in    ATTRIBUTE_NAME;
                              VALUE : in out LIST_TYPE);
procedure GET_NODE_ATTRIBUTE (NODE   : in    NODE_TYPE;
                              ATTRIB : in    ATTRIBUTE_NAME;
                              VALUE : in out LIST_TYPE);

procedure GET_PATH_ATTRIBUTE (NAME   : in    NAME_STRING;
                             ATTRIB : in    ATTRIBUTE_NAME;
                             VALUE : in out LIST_TYPE);
procedure GET_PATH_ATTRIBUTE (BASE     : in    NODE_TYPE;
                             KEY       : in    RELATIONSHIP_KEY;
                             RELATION : in    RELATION_NAME: = DOT;
                             ATTRIB    : in    ATTRIBUTE_NAME;
                             VALUE    : inout LIST_TYPE);

procedure NODE_ATTRIBUTE_ITERATE (ITERATOR : in out ATTRIBUTE_ITERATOR;
                                 NAME     : in    NAME_STRING;
                                 PATTERN : in    ATTRIBUTE_PATTERN
                                                  : = "*");

procedure NODE_ATTRIBUTE_ITERATE (ITERATOR : in out ATTRIBUTE_ITERATOR;
                                 NODE     : in    NODE_TYPE;
                                 PATTERN : in    ATTRIBUTE_PATTERN
                                                  : = "*");

procedure PATH_ATTRIBUTE_ITERATE  (ITERATOR : in out ATTRIBUTE_ITERATOR;
                                  NAME     : NAME_STRING;
                                  PATTERN : ATTRIBUTE_PATTERN
                                                  : = "*");

procedure PATH_ATTRIBUTE_ITERATE (ITERATOR : in out ATTRIBUTE_ITERATOR;
                                 BASE     : in    NODE_TYPE;
                                 KEY       : in    RELATIONSHIP_KEY;
                                 RELATION : in    RELATION_NAME
                                                  : = DOT;
                                 PATTERN  :in    ATTRIBUTE_PATTERN
                                                  : = "*");
```

```
    function MORE (ITERATOR : ATTRIBUTE_ITERATOR) return BOOLEAN;

    procedure GET_NEXT (ITERATOR : in out ATTRIBUTE_ITERATOR;
                        ATTRIB    :    out ATTRIBUTE_NAME;
                        VALUE     : in out LIST_TYPE);

    --  Exceptions

private
    type ATTRIBUTE_ITERATOR is (IMPLEMENTOR_WILL_DEFINE);
    --  implementation-dependent
end ATTRIBUTES;


generic
package ACCESS_CONTROL is

    subtype PRIVILEGE_SPECIFICATION is STRING;

    procedure SET_ACCESS_CONTROL (NODE        : in NODE_TYPE;
                                  GROUP_NODE : in NODE_TYPE;
                                  GRANT       : in PRIVILEGE_SPECIFICATION);
    procedure SET_ACCESS_CONTROL (NAME        : in NAME_STRING;
                                  GROUP_NAME : in NAME_STRING;
                                  GRANT       : in PRIVILEGE_SPECIFICATION);

    function IS_GRANTED (OBJECT_NODE: in NODE_TYPE;
                         PRIVILEGE   : in NAME_STRING) return BOOLEAN;

    function IS_GRANTED (OBJECT_NAME: in NAME_STRING;
                         PRIVILEGE   : in NAME_STRING) return BOOLEAN;

    procedure ADOPT (GROUP_NODE: in NODE_TYPE);
    procedure ADOPT (GROUP_NAME: in NAME_STRING);

end ACCESS_CONTROL;

generic
package STRUCTURAL_NODES is

    procedure CREATE_NODE (NAME   : in NAME_STRING;
                           FORM   : in FORM_STRING := "";
                           ACCESS : in FORM_STRING := "";
                           LEVEL  : in FORM_STRING: = "");
    procedure CREATE_NODE (BASE     : in NODE_TYPE;
                           KEY      : in RELATIONSHIP_KEY;
                           RELATION : in RELATION_NAME := DOT;
                           FORM     : in FORM_STRING := "";
```

```
                              ACCESS    : in FORM_STRING := "";
                              LEVEL     : in FORM_STRING: = "");
      procedure CREATE_NODE (NODE    : in out NODE_TYPE;
                              NAME   : in     NAME_STRING;
                              FORM   : in     FORM_STRING := "";
                              ACCESS : in     FORM_STRING := "";
                              LEVEL  : in     FORM_STRING: = "");
      procedure CREATE_NODE (NODE       : in out NODE_TYPE;
                              BASE     : in    NODE_TYPE;
                              KEY      : in    RELATIONSHIP_KEY;
                              RELATION : in    RELATION_NAME := DOT;
                              FORM     : in    FORM_STRING := "";
                              ACCESS   : in    FORM_STRING := "";
                              LEVEL    : in    FORM_STRING: = "");

end STRUCTURAL_NODES;


generic
package INTERACTIVE_IO is

    type INTERACTIVE_TERMINAL is limited private;
    type CURSOR_POSITION is
        record
            LINE     : POSITIVE;
            COLUMN : POSITIVE;
        end record;

    procedure ASSOCIATE (TERMINAL : in out INTERACTIVE_TERMINAL;
                         INFILE    : in    CAIS_FILE_TYPE;
                         OUTFILE   : in    CAIS_FILE_TYPE);

    procedure SET_LOG (TERMINAL : in out INTERACTIVE_TERMINAL;
                       LOG_FILE : in    CAIS_FILE_TYPE);

    function LOG (TERMINAL : in interactive_TERMINAL)
              return CAIS_FILE_TYPE;

    procedure SET_CURSOR (TERMINAL : in out INTERACTIVE_TERMINAL;
                          POSITION : in    CURSOR_POSITION);

    function CURSOR (TERMINAL : in INTERACTIVE_TERMINAL)
             return CURSOR_POSITION;

    function SIZE (TERMINAL : in INTERACTIVE_TERMINAL)
             return CURSOR_POSITION;

    procedure UPDATE (TERMINAL : in out INTERACTIVE_TERMINAL);
```

239

```
procedure SET_ECHO (TERMINAL : in out INTERACTIVE_TERMINAL;
                    TO        : in    BOOLEAN := TRUE);

function ECHO (TERMINAL : in INTERACTIVE_TERMINAL) return BOOLEAN;

procedure SET_PROMPT (TERMINAL : in INTERACTIVE_TERMINAL;
                      TO        : in STRING);

function PROMPT (TERMINAL : in INTERACTIVE_TERMINAL) return STRING;

--   Exceptions

private
    type INTERACTIVE_TERMINAL is (IMPLEMENTOR_WILL_DEFINE);
    --   implementation-dependent
end INTERACTIVE_IO;

generic
package PROCESS_CONTROL is

    subtype  RESULTS_STRING is LIST_TYPE;
    subtype  PARAMETER_LIST is LIST_TYPE;

    UNIQUE_CHILD_KEY : STRING renames LATEST_KEY;

    procedure SPAWN_PROCESS
                (FILE_NODE_HANDLE   : in    NAME_STRING;
                 INPUT_PARAMETERS   : in    PARAMETER_LIST;
                 NEW_NODE_HANDLE   :   out NODE_TYPE;
                 PATH_NAME          : in    NAME_STRING;
                 INPUT_FILE         : in    NAME_STRING;
                 OUTPUT_FILE        : in    NAME_STRING;
                 ERROR_FILE         : in    NAME_STRING;
                 ENVIRONMENT_NODE : in    NAME_STRING
                                            := CURRENT_NODE);

    procedure SPAWN_PROCESS
                (FILE_NODE_HANDLE   : in    NAME_STRING;
                 INPUT_PARAMETERS   : in    PARAMETER_LIST;
                 NEW_NODE_HANDLE   : in out NODE_TYPE;
                 PARENT_NODE_HANDLE: in    NODE_TYPE;
                 KEY                : in    RELATIONSHIP_KEY
                                            := UNIQUE_CHILD_KEY;
                 RELATION           : in    RELATION_NAME := DOT;
                 INPUT_FILE         : in    NAME_STRING;
                 OUTPUT_FILE        : in    NAME_STRING;
                 ERROR_FILE         : in    NAME_STRING;
                 ENVIRONMENT_NODE   : in    NAME_STRING
                                            := CURRENT_NODE);
```

```
procedure AWAIT_PROCESS_COMPLETION
            (NODE_HANDLE                    : in    NODE_TYPE;
            RESULTS_RETURNED                :     out RESULTS_STRING;
            PROCESS_COMPLETION_STATUS:      out COMPETITION_STATUS;
            TIME_LIMIT                      : in    DURATION
                                                  := DURATION'LAST);


procedure INVOKE_PROCESS
            (FILE_NODE_HANDLE               : in    NAME_STRING;
            INPUT_PARAMETERS                : in    PARAMETER_LIST;
            PROCESS_RESULTS_RETURNED        :    out RESULTS_STRING;
            PROCESS_COMPLETION_STATUS:      out COMPLETION_STATUS;
            PATH_NAME                       : in    NAME_STRING;
            INPUT_FILE                      : in    NAME_STRING;
            OUTPUT_FILE                     : in    NAME_STRING;
            ERROR_FILE                      : in    NAME_STRING;
            ENVIRONMENT_NODE                : in    NAME_STRING
                                                  := CURRENT_NODE;
            TIME_LIMIT                      : in    DURATION
                                                  := DURATION'LAST);


procedure INVOKE_PROCESS
            (FILE_NODE_HANDLE               : in    NAME_STRING;
            INPUT_PARAMETERS                : in    PARAMETER_LIST;
            PROCESS_RESULTS_RETURNED        : in out RESULTS_STRING;
            PROCESS_COMPLETION_STATUS:      out COMPLETION_STATUS;
            PARENT_NODE_HANDLE              : in    NODE_TYPE;
            KEY                             : in    RELATIONSHIP_KEY
                                                  := UNIQUE_CHILD_KEY;
            RELATION                        : in    RELATION_NAME := DOT;
            INPUT_FILE                      : in    NAME_STRING;
            OUTPUT_FILE                     : in    NAME_STRING;
            ERROR_FILE                      : in    NAME_STRING;
            ENVIRONMENT_NODE                : in    NAME_STRING
                                                  := CURRENT_NODE;
            TIME_LIMIT                      : in    DURATION
                                                  := DURATION'LAST);


procedure APPEND_RESULTS (RESULTS : in  RESULTS_STRING);
procedure WRITE_RESULTS   (RESULTS : in  RESULTS_STRING);

procedure GET_RESULTS (NODE_HANDLE : in    NODE_TYPE;
                       RESULTS      : in out RESULTS_STRING);
procedure GET_RESULTS (PATH_NAME    : in    NAME_STRING;
                       RESULTS      : in out RESULTS_STRING);

procedue GET_PARAMETERS (PARAMETERS : in out PARAMETER_LIST);
```

241

```
        procedure ABORT_PROCESS (PATH_NAME    : in NAME_STRING);
        procedure ABORT_PROCESS (NODE_HANDLE : in NODE_TYPE);
        procedure ABORT_PROCESS (PATH_NAME    : in NAME_STRING;
                                 RESULTS       : in RESULTS_STRING);
        procedure ABORT_PROCESS (NODE_HANDLE : in NODE_TYPE;
                                 RESULTS       : in RESULTS_STRING);

        procedure SUSPEND_PROCESS (PATH_NAME    : in NAME_STRING);
        procedure SUSPEND_PROCESS (NODE_HANDLE : in NODE_TYPE);

        procedure RESUME_PROCESS (PATH_NAME    : in NAME_STRING);
        procedure RESUME_PROCESS (NODE_HANDLE : in NODE_TYPE);

        function STATE_OF_PROCESS (PATH_NAME    : in NAME_STRING)
                                  return PROCESS_STATUS;
        function STATE_OF_PROCESS (NODE_HANDLE : in NODE_TYPE)
                                  return PROCESS_STATUS;

        function JOB_INPUT_FILE    return NAME_STRING;
        function JOB_OUTPUT_FILE return NAME_STRING;
        function JOB_ERROR_FILE    return NAME_STRING;

        --  Exceptions

end process_CONTROL;

generic
package PROCESS_INTERRUPTS is

        subtype INTERRUPT_NAME      is STRING;
        type    INTERRUPT_RESPONSE is (IGNORE, AWAKE, HOLD);

        procedure SIGNAL  (NODE_HANDLE : in NODE_TYPE;
                           INTERRUPT      : in INTERRUPT_NAME);

        procedure SIGNAL  (PATH_NAME : in NAME_STRING;
                           INTERRUPT  : in INTERRUPT_NAME);

        procedure SET_RESPONSE (INTERRUPT  : in INTERRUPT_NAME;
                                RESPONSE   : in INTERRUPT_RESPONSE;
                                TIME_LIMIT : in DURATION := DURATION'LAST);

        function RESPONSE (INTERRUPT : in INTERRUPT_NAME)
                          return INTERUPT_RESPONSE;

        --  Exceptions

end PROCESS_INTERRUPTS;
```

```
generic
package FILE_MANAGEMENT is

    type FILE_MODE is (IN_NEED_OF_DEFINITION);

    procedure CREATE (FILE          : in out CAIS_FILE_TYPE;
                      MODE          : in    FILE_MODE;
                      BASE          : in    NODE_TYPE;
                      KEY           : in    RELATIONSHIP_KEY;
                      RELATION      : in    RELATION_NAME;
                      FORM          : in    FORM_STRING := "");

    procedure OPEN   (FILE          : in out CAIS_FILE_TYPE;
                      MODE          : in    FILE_MODE;
                      BASE          : in    NODE_TYPE;
                      KEY           : in    RELATIONSHIP_KEY;
                      RELATION      : in    RELATION_NAME;
                      FORM          : in    FORM_STRING := "");

    procedure OPEN   (FILE          : in out CAIS_FILE_TYPE;
                      MODE          : in    FILE_MODE;
                      NODE_HANDLE   : in    NODE_TYPE;
                      FORM          : in    FORM_STRING := "");

    procedure OPEN_NODE (NODE_HANDLE : in out NODE_TYPE;
                         FILE         : in    CAIS_FILE_TYPE;

end FILE_MANAGEMENT;

generic
package TEXT_IO is

    subtype COUNT is POSITIVE;

    procedure SET_LINE_LENGTH  (FILE : in CAIS_FILE_TYPE;
                                TO  : in COUNT);
    procedure SET_LINE_LENGTH  (TO  : in COUNT);

    procedure SET_PAGE_LENGTH (FILE : in CAIS_FILE_TYPE;
                               TO  : in COUNT);
    procedure SET_PAGE_LENGTH (TO  : in COUNT);

    procedure NEW_LINE (FILE      : in CAIS_FILE_TYPE;
                        SPACING : in POSITIVE := 1);
    procedure NEW_LINE (SPACING : in POSITIVE := 1);

    procedure NEW_PAGE (FILE : in CAIS_FILE_TYPE);
    procedure NEW_PAGE;
```

243

```
        procedure SET_ERROR (FILE : in CAIS_FILE_TYPE);

        function STANDARD_ERROR return NAME_STRING;

end TEXT_IO;



generic
package TERMINAL_SUPPORT is

        procedure OPEN (TERMINAL : in out TERMINAL_TYPE;
                        NAME     : in      NAME_STRING;
                        CLASS    : in      TERMINAL_CLASS := SCROLL);
        procedure OPEN (TERMINAL : in out TERMINAL_TYPE;
                        BASE     : in      NODE_TYPE;
                        KEY      : in      RELATIONSHIP_KEY;
                        RELATION : in      RELATION_NAME := DOT;
                        CLASS    : in      TERMINAL_CLASS := SCROLL);

        procedure CLOSE (TERMINAL : in out TERMINAL_TYPE);

        procedure RESET  (TERMINAL : in out TERMINAL_TYPE;
                          CLASS     : in      TERMINAL_CLASS);
        procedure RESET  (TERMINAL : in out TERMINAL_TYPE);

        function CLASS     (TERMINAL : in TERMINAL_TYPE) return TERMINAL_CLASS;
        function FORM     (TERMINAL : in TERMINAL_TYPE) return FORM_STRING;
        function IS_OPEN (TERMINAL : in TERMINAL_TYPE) return BOOLEAN;

        procedure SET_POSITION (TERMINAL : in out TERMINAL_TYPE;
                                POSITION : in     ACTIVE_POSITION);

        function POSITION (TERMINAL : in TERMINAL_TYPE)
                   return ACTIVE_POSITION;

        function SIZE       (TERMINAL : in TERMINAL_TYPE)
                   return ACTIVE_POSITION;

    --  Exceptions

end TERMINAL_SUPPORT;

generic
package SCROLL_TERMINAL is

        procedure SET_TAB     (TERMINAL : in out TERMINAL_TYPE);
        procedure CLEAR_TAB (TERMINAL : in out TERMINAL_TYPE);
```

244

```
procedure TAB          (TERMINAL : in out TERMINAL_TYPE;
                        COUNT    : in    POSITIVE := 1);

procedure NEW_LINE  (TERMINAL : in out TERMINAL_TYPE;
                        COUNT    : in    POSITIVE := 1);

procedure NEW_PAGE  (TERMINAL : in out TERMINAL_TYPE;
                        COUNT    : in    POSITIVE := 1);

procedure PUT (TERMINAL : in out TERMINAL_TYPE;
            ITEM      : in    CHARACTER);
procedure PUT (TERMINAL : in out TERMINAL_TYPE;
            ITEM      : in    STRING);

procedure UPDATE (TERMINAL : in out TERMINAL_TYPE);

procedure GET (TERMINAL : in out TERMINAL_TYPE;
            ITEM      :    out CHARACTER);
procedure GET (TERMINAL : in out TERMINAL_TYPE;
            ITEM      :    out STRING);
procedure GET (TERMINAL : in out TERMINAL_TYPE;
            ITEM      :    out STRING);
            LAST      :    out NATURAL);

procedure SET_ECHO (TERMINAL : in out TERMINAL_TYPE;
                    TO       : in    BOOLEAN := TRUE);

function ECHO          (TERMINAL : in TERMINAL_TYPE)
                        return BOOLEAN;

procedure BELL         (TERMINAL : in out TERMINAL_TYPE);

--  Exceptions

end SCROLL_TERMINAL;

generic
package PAGE_TERMINAL is

    type SELECT_ENUMERATION is (FROM_ACTIVE_POSITION_TO_END,
                                FROM_START_TO_ACTIVE_POSITION,
                                ALL_POSITIONS);

    type GRAPHIC_RENDITION_ENUMERATION is
                        (PRIMARY_RENDITION,
                        BOLD,
                        FAINT,
                        UNDERSCORE,
```

```
                                        SLOW_BLINK,
                                        RAPID_BLINK,
                                        REVERSE_IMAGE);

    procedure DELETE_CHARACTER (TERMINAL : in out TERMINAL_TYPE;
                                COUNT    : in    POSITIVE := 1);

    procedure DELETE_LINE      (TERMINAL : in out TERMINAL_TYPE;
                                COUNT    : in    POSITIVE := 1);

    procedure ERASE_CHARACTER  (TERMINAL : in out TERMINAL_TYPE;
                                COUNT    : in    POSITIVE := 1);

    procedure ERASE_IN_DISPLAY (TERMINAL  : in out TERMINAL_TYPE;
                                SELECTION : SELECT_ENUMERATION);
    procedure ERASE_IN_LINE    (TERMINAL  : in out TERMINAL_TYPE;
                                SELECTION : SELECT_ENUMERATION);

    procedure INSERT_CHARACTER (TERMINAL : in out TERMINAL_TYPE;
                                COUNT    : in    POSITIVE := 1);
    procedure INSERT_LINE      (TERMINAL : in out TERMINAL_TYPE;
                                COUNT    : in    POSITIVE := 1);

    procedure SELECT_GRAPHIC_RENDITION
                    (TERMINAL  : in out TERMINAL_TYPE;
                     SELECTION : in    GRAPHIC_RENDITION_ENUMERATION);

    procedure SET_TAB   (TERMINAL : in out TERMINAL_TYPE);
    procedure CLEAR_TAB (TERMINAL : in out TERMINAL_TYPE);

    procedure TAB       (TERMINAL : in out TERMINAL_TYPE;
                         COUNT    in    POSITIVE := 1);

    procedure PUT (TERMINAL : in out TERMINAL_TYPE;
                   ITEM     : in    CHARACTER);
    procedure PUT (TERMINAL : in out TERMINAL_TYPE;
                   ITEM     : in    STRING);

    procedure UPDATE (TERMINAL : in out TERMINAL_TYPE);

    procedure GET (TERMINAL : in out TERMINAL_TYPE;
                   ITEM     : in    CHARACTER);
    procedure GET (TERMINAL : in out TERMINAL_TYPE;
                   ITEM     : in    STRING);
    procedure GET (TERMINAL : in out TERMINAL_TYPE;
                   ITEM     : in    STRING;
                   LAST     :    out NATURAL);
```

```
    procedure SET_ECHO (TERMINAL : in out TERMINAL_TYPE;
                        TO        : in    BOOLEAN := TRUE);

    function ECHO       (TERMINAL : in TERMINAL_TYPE)
                        return BOOLEAN;

    procedure BELL      (TERMINAL : in out TERMINAL_TYPE);
    --  Exceptions

end PAGE_TERMINAL;

generic
    type TERMINATION_KEY_RANGE is range <>;
package FORM_TERMINAL is
    type AREA_INTENSITY   is (NONE, NORMAL, HIGH);
    type AREA_PROTECTION is (UNPROTECTED, PROTECTED);
    type AREA_INPUT       is (GRAPHIC_CHARACTERS, NUMERICS, ALPHABETICS);
    type AREA_VALUE       is (NO_FILL, FILL_WITH_ZEROES, FILL_WITH_SPACES);

    procedure DEFINE_QUALIFIED_AREA
                    (TERMINAL   : in out TERMINAL_TYPE;
                     INTENSITY  : in     AREA_INTENSITY    := NORMAL;
                     PROTECTION : in     AREA_PROTECTION := PROTECTED;
                     INPUT      : in     AREA_INPUT
                                              := GRAPHIC_CHARACTERS;
                     VALUE      : in     AREA_VALUE        := NO_FILL);

    procedure CLEAR_QUALIFIED_AREA (TERMINAL : in out TERMINAL_TYPE);

    procedure TAB (TERMINAL : in out TERMINAL_TYPE);
    procedure PUT (TERMINAL : in out TERMINAL_TYPE;
                   ITEM     : in     CHARACTER);
    procedure PUT (TERMINAL : in out TERMINAL_TYPE;
                   ITEM     : in     STRING);

    procedure GET (TERMINAL : in out TERMINAL_TYPE);
                   ITEM     :    out CHARACTER);
    procedure GET (TERMINAL : in out TERMINAL_TYPE;
                   ITEM     :    out STRING);

    procedure ERASE_AREA      (TERMINAL : in out TERMINAL_TYPE);
    procedure ERASE_DISPLAY   (TERMINAL : in out TERMINAL_TYPE);
    procedure ACTIVATE_FORM   (TERMINAL : in out TERMINAL_TYPE);

    function IS_FORM_UPDATED (TERMINAL : in TERMINAL_TYPE)
                                  return BOOLEAN;
    function AREA_QUALIFIER_REQUIRES_SPACE (TERMINAL : in TERMINAL_TYPE)
                                              return BOOLEAN;
```

```
        function TERMINATION_KEY  (TERMINAL : in TERMINAL_TYPE)
                                  return TERMINATION_KEY_RANGE;

        --  Exceptions

end FORM_TERMINAL;

private
        type NODE_TYPE       is (IMPLEMENTOR_WILL_DEFINE);
        type TEXT_TYPE       is (IMPLEMENTOR_WILL_DEFINE);
        type TERMINAL_TYPE is (IMPLEMENTOR_WILL_DEFINE);
        type CAIS_FILE_TYPE  is (IMPLEMENTOR_WILL_DEFINE);
end CAIS;
```

Index

Abort 97, 109

Absolute pathnames 124

Access control 58, 116

Ada language reference manual 11, 13–15, 20, 24–25, 28, 83, 90, 157, 168, 171, 175

Address 21, 23, 25, 158, 167, 189

Archive 44, 143, 150–151, 153

Assembler 143, 151

Assignment 16–17, 50, 93, 119, 126–127, 138, 199

Attributes 18, 20, 22, 60, 93–94, 117, 128, 132–135, 138, 140, 142–143, 145, 152

Background 69, 78, 83, 87, 95, 97, 100, 131

Binding 16, 18, 23, 50, 130, 158–161, 174

Break 91, 197–198, 200

CAIS 116, 122, 214–216, 218–221, 224

Certification 195–196, 220

Command language 59, 67, 77, 82, 89, 101, 206, 210, 226

Communication 7, 30, 41, 81, 105, 183, 188–189, 197, 207, 215, 221

Compiler 5–6, 10–11, 13–14, 16–17, 33, 85, 143, 152, 159–161, 164–167, 169, 172, 174, 182, 196, 225

Configuration management 8–9, 29, 113, 131–132, 140, 165, 193, 196, 207, 221, 224

Continuation 50, 71, 90, 93, 98, 117, 158, 227

Control 5, 7, 9, 11, 14, 16–17, 22–23, 28–31, 33–34, 40, 42–44, 50, 53, 55, 58, 61, 74, 81–85, 89–93, 96–99, 103, 105–107, 116, 118, 133–136, 138, 144–147, 157–159, 169, 181–184, 187–189, 196–198, 201, 205–206, 208–209, 213, 215, 225

Correctness 194–197, 199, 201

CPCI 191–192, 219–220

Create 24–25, 41, 43, 58, 62–63, 65, 67–69, 75, 78–79, 82–83, 96, 99, 107–109, 115–116, 119, 121, 124, 127–128, 132–133,

(Create continued)
135, 137–139, 143, 145–146, 152, 165–166, 170, 172, 178, 183–184, 187–188, 190

Data base 29, 39, 41–45, 49–50, 60–62, 74, 87, 95, 99, 104, 106, 111, 113–118, 120, 123, 130–135, 137, 142, 151, 172, 206–207, 212, 214
Data structures 12
Debugging 151, 168, 174, 201, 225–226
Declarative 48–49
Delete 106, 129, 138, 143, 146
Denotational approach (to semantics) 48–51, 227
Design language 221–222
Design review 193–195, 220
Devices 7, 30, 55–56, 86–87, 103, 105, 107, 109, 114, 116–117, 128, 132–133, 158, 172–173, 208–210, 213, 215
Diagnostics 45, 79, 164, 167, 170
Diana 13, 26, 167, 225
Directory 60, 63, 74, 108, 138, 178, 189, 212
Distributed programming 144, 189
Documentation 9, 93
Domain 28, 39, 49–50, 85, 89, 116–117, 158, 182
Dynamic analysis 42, 196–197

Editor 63–64, 66, 103–107, 109, 115, 179, 209–210
Embedded computer 3, 6–7, 9–10, 26, 85, 212
Environment 14–15, 27–28, 37, 40–41, 50, 84, 92, 97, 99, 109, 117, 157–159, 209, 223, 225–226
Evaluation 50, 192–196, 200, 219–220, 224

Exceptions 22–23, 26, 90–91, 158–159, 173, 177–179, 189–190
Executing 5, 14, 50, 96–97, 157, 159, 165, 185, 197
Export 73–74, 143, 151, 159, 167, 173–175, 177, 179, 189, 197–198, 211, 214, 221

Files 8, 24, 60, 65, 67, 72, 74–79, 93 to 94, 107–108, 114, 116, 118, 129, 132–133, 135, 138–147, 151–152, 164–167, 170, 172–173, 176–179, 185–190, 207, 213, 215
Foreground 69, 83, 95, 97, 99
Format 7, 65, 107, 144, 151, 159, 167, 173, 221
Fortran 17, 27, 171–174
Frequency 41, 165, 173–174, 197

Get 59–62, 67, 71, 74–76, 92, 129, 137–138, 143, 146, 213

Help facilities 59, 149–150, 152
Hierarchical organization 30, 58, 62, 114, 116–119, 122, 126, 129–131, 168, 175, 179
History attributes 43, 132, 170
Host 9, 24, 30–31, 33–37, 55–58, 79, 81–82, 158, 173, 197–198, 205–207, 210, 212, 214, 216–218

Import 113, 143, 150, 152, 163, 171–172, 174, 221
Incomplete programming 179
Input 4–5, 12, 15, 24, 35, 41, 67, 76–78, 84, 86–87, 90–93, 95–96, 105, 107, 109, 152, 173, 182, 196, 207, 209–210, 213
Inspection 164
Integrated 28, 39–40, 103, 107–109, 167, 192, 209, 223, 225

Interaction 56, 82, 105, 182, 207–209, 214, 224

Interactive tools 44, 55–56, 82, 87, 100, 103, 143, 168, 197, 208–209, 212–213, 224, 226

Interfaces 11, 17, 28–31, 33–37, 39, 44–45, 50–51, 81–82, 85, 103, 117, 152, 168, 171, 192–193, 195, 203, 205–214, 216–219, 224–225

Interlisp 28, 37, 85, 209, 227

Interoperability 55, 193, 205, 207–208, 210, 217–220

Interrupts 7, 17, 91, 97, 100, 158, 189, 197, 215

Invocation 63, 65, 68, 83, 96–97, 103, 124, 128, 138, 159, 170, 173–174, 209, 214, 225

Kapse 31, 33–37, 82, 108, 205–220, 222, 224–225

Key 47, 56, 85, 87, 90–91, 126, 129–130, 133–135, 194, 205, 209, 220

Layered model 30–31, 81, 114, 117, 195, 205

Lexical units 86, 89–91, 107, 167

Library 14–15, 33, 66, 68–69, 74–75, 141–147, 151–152, 157, 159, 164, 166–167, 169–172, 176, 179, 187–188, 190, 211, 214, 216

Life cycle 9, 12, 17, 29, 31, 39–40, 109, 193, 195–196

Link 30, 56, 73–74, 81, 127, 142, 151–152, 167, 170, 172, 177–179

Linker 33, 143, 152, 159, 169–171, 177–178, 187–189, 196

List 61, 63, 65, 69–70, 76–78, 92, 94, 98, 135, 138, 143, 146, 199–200

Login 58, 79, 99, 109

Logout 78, 99, 109

Machine code insertions 24, 167

Mail 9, 71, 73, 109, 208

Main program 14–15, 26, 65–66, 74, 86, 170, 172, 177

Maintenance 3, 8, 15, 44, 221

Mapse 33–35, 42, 79, 82, 89–90, 96, 99, 103, 107, 109, 207, 209

Memory 5, 16, 87, 157–159, 169–170, 173, 188

Message-passing 183

Mouse 86, 109, 209

Naming 18, 23–24, 114, 117, 120–121, 123, 127, 133, 144, 146, 206–207

Node handle 120–121, 123

Node model 49, 79, 117, 130

Object 12, 30, 36, 41–43, 45–46, 48–50, 55, 60–62, 64–65, 67, 73–74, 76, 79, 81–83, 86–87, 91, 93, 95, 98–99, 104, 106–107, 113–118, 120, 123, 126–127, 131–137, 139, 142–143, 151, 169–170, 172–173, 183–185, 212, 214–215

Operating system 28, 31, 33–35, 37, 45, 79, 160–161, 205–208, 210, 217–218, 227

Operational approach (to semantics) 13, 49

Optimization 17, 40–41, 164, 174

Output 4, 12, 15, 24, 41, 66, 73, 86–87, 92, 95–96, 114, 141, 152, 159, 172, 178–179, 188–189, 207, 209, 213–214

Overlay 169–171, 188

Packages 11–12, 66, 159, 179, 188, 212–214, 217–219, 222

Paging 173

Parallel computation 3, 27, 181–182, 184

Partition 43, 60, 116, 118, 129, 136, 138
Pathname 107, 122–128, 130, 134, 142, 164
Pipes 96
Portability 20, 29–30
Pragmas 15–17, 22, 164, 167
Pragmatics 13, 26, 167, 210, 213
Predefined language environment 12, 15–16, 22, 99, 142, 159, 161, 167
Pretty-printer 107
Primary pathnames 126–129, 134
Print 42, 56, 95–96, 116, 152
Procedural 11–12, 48–49, 58
Process 49, 58, 79, 96, 99, 108, 171, 183, 185, 189, 215
Programming language 4–6, 26–27, 85, 221, 223, 227
Programming structures 12
Programming support 3, 27–28, 31, 226
Project mangement 10, 43, 113, 115–116, 119, 131, 136–137
Protocols 30, 33, 44, 221

Quality assurance 41, 168, 191–194, 221

Read 67, 71–72, 77, 98, 104, 106, 109, 122–123, 134–135, 172
Redirection 78, 92, 95
Relation 71, 73, 117–118, 120–123, 126, 129–130, 135–136, 139
Relationship 36, 120–121, 127
Relationship key 121–123, 126, 129
Relative pathnames 124, 137
Remote tasks 169–170, 189
Rendezvous 83, 183–184
Representation 6, 23, 41, 49, 89, 115, 123, 143, 174, 227
Requirements documents 3

Resource allocation 43, 83, 169–171, 182–184, 188
Resume 83, 97–99, 197
Revision 9, 115–116, 133, 139–140, 152
Running 5, 160, 165
Runtime support 155, 157, 159, 161, 163, 168–169, 174, 188–189, 211–212, 221

Script 67, 76–78, 82–86, 95–96, 98–99, 101, 109, 134
Secondary pathnames 127, 130
Security 120–121, 134
Semantics 13–14, 24–26, 28, 34, 42, 47–51, 58, 85–86, 90, 93, 130, 151, 159, 161, 181–182, 191, 206, 208, 213, 217–218, 226
Separate compilation 15, 26, 33, 141, 143, 175
Separator tool 187, 189–190, 221
Software components 192–193
Software engineering 8, 28, 113–114, 168, 225–226
Software tools 28–29
Spawning processes 58, 84, 87, 108–109, 183–184
Special characters 87, 92, 106
Standardization 4, 6, 14, 27, 30, 36, 47, 50, 67, 77, 79, 85–87, 93–96, 98, 179, 194–195, 205–210, 214, 216–220, 223–225
Static analysis 196
Statistics 41, 43, 164–165, 167
Stoneman 3–4, 6–9, 27–28, 30, 33, 42, 44–45, 51, 81–82, 85, 87, 101, 103, 107, 109, 113–114, 117, 132, 138, 146, 173, 196, 205, 207, 209, 213, 216, 219–220
Storage 4, 15–16, 18, 22–23, 34, 104, 113, 151, 169, 171–172
Store 25, 50, 92, 99, 116, 158

Stub 152, 178–179
Subcommands 73, 143, 151
Subunit 142–144, 175–176, 178, 185
Suspend 83, 96–99, 108, 198
Syntax 13, 28, 50, 82, 85–86, 89, 108, 122, 151, 167, 199, 206, 213, 222

Target 9, 14, 17, 22, 37, 40–41, 56, 69, 142–143, 151–152, 158–160, 166–171, 173–174, 177, 182–185, 191, 197–198, 200, 206–209, 212, 218, 227
Task 13, 15, 17, 83, 168–169, 181–185, 187–188, 196, 209
Task scheduling 173, 183, 196
Terminal 42, 56, 79, 83, 86–87, 90, 95, 105, 209, 212–215
Terminate 8, 15, 24, 64, 70–71, 78, 91, 95, 97, 99, 106
Test 13, 177–178, 192–195, 201, 219–220
Time-sharing 183

Timing 17, 22, 167, 173–174, 197
Topology 169–171, 183, 187, 205
Transportability 55, 81–82, 184, 205, 207–208, 210, 217–220
Turing machine 4–5, 9, 24

Undefinitions 14, 157
Undo command 152–153

Validation 6, 8, 13–14, 195, 225–226
Variation 9, 115–116, 138–140
Verification 8, 191–192, 195–196, 219–220
Version 43, 63, 66, 74–77, 115–116, 133–134, 138–140, 143, 145, 147, 152, 223–224

Windows 105–109, 209–210
With clause 167, 169, 177, 212
Write 6, 72, 84–85, 101, 126, 134

Zonk–11 160